I wish to acknowledge the support of the following sponsors:

Durex Condoms —For the frequent loan of Richard the Dick costume, and for sponsoring everything I've ever done.

The Canadian Men's Clinic—Thanks to Jody and Carol Bresgi
Special thanks to Lillyann, and Wallace Studio's Toronto. The best television studio in the world!

Cover illustration by David Shackleton
Some inside illustrations by Scott Fiander

Special thanks to Lisa Duncan and Gregg Molyneaux at The Tri-Co Group Inc. for all their help on the production of this book.

Special thanks to my listeners. Those fun, engaging, amazing people who interact with me on the air. Thanks, this book is for you!

Find out about Sue McGarvie, International Sex and Relationship Expert and syndicated radio host of "Sex with Sue". Check out the website www.sexwithsue.com for Sue's speaking schedule.

If you suggest this book to your friends, have them e-mail me directly at sexwithsue@rogers.com. For the referral, I'll send you a special report called, "Tickle me with the Feather Duster..." *things you can find around the house to keep your sex life fun and intriguing.* **I'll also put you on the list for a special coupon towards my next book out soon, Giant Phalluses: Everything you wanted to know about PENIS SIZE!**

Quivering Jello: How to Have Mind-Blowing, Toe Curling Orgasms.

This book is intended as a reference volume only, not as a medical manual. The information given here is to help you reach better orgasms, but is offered as suggestions only. It is not intended as a substitute for any treatment or information from a medical professional.

Copyright 2003 by SuMac Productions, a division of Romance Communications

Content copyright by Sue McGarvie

All rights reserved. No part of this publication may be reproduced or transmitted in any form or by any means, electronic or mechanical, including photocopying and recording of any type without the express written permission of the author and publisher.

Printed in Canada 2003

SuMac Productions, a division of Romance Communication.
99 Holland Ave., Suite 105,
Ottawa, Ontario Canada
K1Y 0Y1
(613) 725-2789   www.sexwithsue.com
Sexwithsue@rogers.com

Cataloguing Data
McGarvie, Sue, 1966-
Quivering Jello: How to Have Mind Blowing, Toe Curling Orgasms!

1st ed.
Includes index
ISBN 0-9683612-0-X

1. Sexual Fulfillment.
2. Sexual excitement.
3. Men and Women– Sexual behavior I. Title

HQ 21.M117 2003   613.9'6   C03-900412-0

QUIVERING JELLO:
How to Have Mind-Blowing, Toe Curling Orgasms

Mmmm, OhhH, Yes… More…Harder, Ahhhh….!!!!!

Table of Contents

Introduction	*5*
Anatomy 101 *Male and Female*	*15*
Orgasms Defined *A different kind of Orgasm* *The G-Spot* *The History of the G-Spot* *Finding the G-Spot* *G-Spot Mechanics*	*24*
Trouble Shooting Orgasm Difficulties *Keegal Exercise and Wonders* *Female Ejaculation* *Prostate Problems* *Her Orgasm*	*40*
Sex Toys	*63*
Wall Socket Sex *The P-Spot* *Tantric Sex* *Other Types of Orgasms* *Extended Sexual Orgasm*	*69*
Orgasm Letters *Letters from Listeners* *Tips from Sue*	*78*
Putting It All Together	*106*
About the Author	*110*

Quivering Jello: How to have Amazing Orgasms that turn you to mush!

The sensation of orgasm is one of life's true pleasures. It releases sexual tension, causes pleasurable endorphins to course through our bodies, can cause the earth to move, and can at least put a smile on our faces.

However, the comprehensive Sex in America Study published in 1996 suggests that close to 12% of women have never reached an orgasm. This sad statistic represents millions of wives, mothers and lovers throughout North America. Women who for the most part have simply not learned about the magic their bodies can perform. Most men when surveyed reach orgasm, but wish they could last longer, have more intense orgasms, and are very interested in learning about pleasing their partners. The other big issue for men around orgasm is whether men can achieve multiple orgasms, or whether this is a sexual myth. Sexuality and reaching orgasm is an important part of our everyday lives.

Sex is a basic need but we collectively spend very little energy, work, or

Did you know that most women (over 85%) have faked an orgasm in their lives. Most women fake to make their partners feel better about their performance.

time thinking about it. In terms of needs, it ranks just behind food, as the second most important thing our bodies need and crave in order to function. Most adults are either having sex, or would like to be having sex. The problem is that with what I call "busy people syndrome," sex moves lower down the priority list behind doing the laundry.

Every study about relationship intimacy since the dawn of time tells us that sex is imperative in keeping us connected with our partners. And orgasms are what keep us interested in sex. Sex is the glue within our relationships. It gives us the feeling of intimacy or the squoogies that "Agrhhh or oomph" in the pit of our stomach when we see our partners. My favorite study was illustrated on the now classic British television series *The Good Sex Guide,* where participating married couples who agreed to abstain from sex for over six months. The researchers discovered that the couples started having marital difficulties and felt like roommates or siblings without the sex. Sex creates intimacy in our relationships.

In North America, a recent trend is that people are deciding to be more

- **Can men achieve Multiple Orgasms?**
- *There's a book called the Multiply Orgasmic Man written by Doug Arama who offers suggestions and specific techniques for separating orgasms from ejaculation. I'll cover some of those tips later in the book!*

sexually open and curious about sex within a monogamous relationship. In a culture still living with AIDS twenty years or more after it arrived with a bang, and with an understanding of how other sexually transmitted diseases are epidemic, the days of "free love" are behind us.

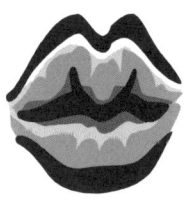

So as a culture we need to find new ways to keep sex exciting, within the confines of a committed relationship. We try new things, and keep the sex hot – some of which we'll explore in this book but we still need to make sure that there is sexual fulfillment, and by that I mean **ORGASMS!!!!**

Sex is what you make it. It can range from a reproductive rubbing of the genitals, an in-out-repeat if-necessary thrusting or it can cause you to have a religious experience where you see stars, experience colors and release fluid, tension and make you believe that all is right with the universe. An exploration of orgasms, a how to primer for both men and women, **Quivering Jello: How to Have Mind-Blowing, Toe Curling Orgasms** will help you put your Ohhh….. in your mmmmmm…....

   I promise that help is within these pages. If you follow the suggestions found in **Quivering Jello: How to Have Mind-Blowing, Toe Curling Orgasms,** you'll be well on your way to knowing about and experiencing the kind of orgasms that I've heard call wall socket sex. They are so powerful you feel like you've been shocked with a zap of electricity.

Find out more about all of this at the coolest website on the planet.
www.sexwithsue.com

When we discuss orgasms we are going to focus on the overall sensation, how to increase the intensity of the pleasure, how to have orgasms come from all over your body instead of just genitally focused, and how to increase the duration of the orgasm. For men the anatomy is pretty straight forward. I've almost never had a guy call me on my radio show and ask what's an orgasm. Even young teenage boys get what an orgasm is because they ejaculate, have wet dreams, and start masturbating early. They call a penis a boy's first and favorite toy. It's out there, and easy to focus on, and statistically, men have fewer orgasm problems.

For women, however, the story is much more complicated. Women have the capacity to achieve multiple orgasms, but for many women having their first orgasm can be a challenge. The three most common sexual problems affecting women are painful intercourse, inability to reach orgasm, and low sex drive. Orgasms, or lack of orgasms, are related to two out of three of these sexual problems. The current research on inhibited sexual desire or low sex drive, shows that many women who aren't interested in sex or claim to have a decreased sex drive have difficulties reaching or worse, have

> **Psst... Most women reach orgasm by oral sex! We like it!**

never experienced an orgasm no matter how hard they've tried.

This book will offer concrete solutions on how to reach orgasms, it will also offer up a huge selection of tips, suggestions, and experiences for reaching the elusive G-spot orgasm. **Quivering Jello: How to Have Mind-Blowing, Toe Curling, Orgasms** will outline the physiology of orgasms, and suggest ways for both men and women to increase the intensity, frequency, types and overall potency

In Summary, Quivering Jello: The Big Book of Orgasms will tell you:

How to have stronger, longer and more frequent orgasms

Everything you'll ever want to know about the G-Spot Orgasm

Male orgasms, Female Orgasms the differences and what you need to know about you and your partner's climax.

Stories, tips and suggestions for reaching your magical, mysterious orgasm

Troubleshooting—things to try if your orgasm is non-existent or difficult to reach

G Spot success letters—real life experiences from listeners who finally, finally, reach the elusive G-Spot orgasm

of the orgasms they are having. I'll spend a lot of time on the G-spot orgasm because it is one of the most confusing topics around orgasms. I would say that problems reaching G-spot and vaginal orgasms are among the most common questions I get as a sex therapist and broadcaster. Finally, we will look at solutions for all of the most common problems that may be inhibiting or decreasing your chances for reaching the Big O. This book should help you reach the orgasms you are struggling

Sue Says: Orgasms feel like having a delicious sneeze! More stories of these kinds of wild explosions at www.sexwithsue.com

 **Most men like a firm touch, where women want to be handled with care!**

with. If it doesn't, and you still can't climax, e-mail me at sexwithsue@rogers.com, include the words **wall socket** in your subject line, and I'll send you some more brainstorming ideas. If you've bought the book, then I am committed to helping.

So, What is an Orgasm?

Basically, an orgasm happens in the body when blood rushes down to the genitals, and because of direct stimulation on the nerve endings, a genital spasm is triggered. This spasm, or series of pulses is known as an orgasm.

In both sexes the nipples get erect, a flush spreads over the stomach, chest and neck, the heart races, blood pressure soars, you break into a sweat and the muscles involuntarily contract.

Masters and Johnson

Men...

In guys, the sensation is usually combined with ejaculation – or the pulsing of the muscles that cause semen to flood out of the penis. What isn't commonly known, is that there is a clear difference between orgasm and ejaculation. It's been proven that the sensation of orgasm can happen without having an ejaculation, and that ejaculation can happen without an orgasm.

As an example, men who have spinal cord injuries can produce semen and ejaculate by a simple electrical stimulation of the prostate gland. They insert a small vibrator, stimulate the prostate in the rectum and voila, you have an ejaculation. That's ejaculation but without the sensation of orgasm, but stay with me and I'll explain how to have an orgasm without ejaculation. You stay hard longer and can have those all night lovemaking sessions!

The joke about how God gave men the ability to pee standing up, and women multiple orgasms will no longer hold true. With enough work, and the right information you too can be Quivering Jello—as the orgasms keep mounting. Keep reading and I'll tell you what the experts with the penises say about becoming a multiply orgasmic man. That's when you last as long as you want, it feels wonderful and you only come when you choose to! YEAH!!!!

The big difference between men and women is that after orgasm men shut down and go through a refractory period that lasts from a few minutes to a couple of days. During that time, men aren't interested in sex, where as women go on to have wave after wave of orgasmic response. As many as 134 in a laboratory setting, if the scientists can count correctly.

> "The first and foremost erogenous zone is in the mind"
>
> Richard Miller, The Magical

Women....
For women the sensation, and mechanics of orgasm are the same, but finding the right spot can be a little

more elusive. For guys it's easy to see the area that's needing to be touched. Just grab the head of the penis and the shaft firmly and start stroking. [For women however, the type of touch that men find stimulating women usually find much to rough.] The nub like structure that is the clitoris hides as many nerve endings in an area the size of your pinky nail as are in the entire penis. No wonder too much direct stimulation can be overwhelming.

" For men pretty much anything works. Apply some friction to the head of the penis and he's happy. Women, on the other hand, become aroused in different places on the body; they respond to different levels of stimulation, different tempos. And they are even variable from one time to the next." Dr. Strassberg, *Sex; A Man's Guide* - page 110.

Where's the explosion?

Physiologically, a woman's orgasm is expressed by multiple cramp-like contractions of the vagina. Her nipples and clitoris begin to swell with dammed up blood, and her uterus (out of sight and the size of her fist) can swell up close to double in size in women who've had children.

Fortunately, it feels better than it sounds.

Both men and women can have as many as 25 of these contractions, but unless the orgasm is off the Richter scale most people have less than ten of these flutters. A really great orgasm can have shock waves, and the spasms can last up to four seconds at their peak. The intensity and length diminish as the orgasm wears on but at its peak, the electrical charge can last two to four seconds of magnified pleasure. There is no universally accepted definition of orgasm, but "written descriptions of orgasm by men and women are indistinguishable from each other." (*Men's Health—Sex: A Man's Guide, page 67*)

Interestingly, all of the changes happening in the body during sexual activity, such as increased blood pressure, rapid breathing, sex flush or rash across the top of the chest, tightening of the anus and genital muscles, darkening of the head of the penis and the inner lips of the vagina, and strong feelings of pleasure that cause euphoria, happen much more intensely during orgasm than during any other phase of sexual excitement. The brain "switches off" and focuses inward, and a person experiencing the orgasm may be tongue tied or incoherent for a moment. It sometimes becomes a religious experience (Oh my God, that feels good!) . The French call this state "Le Petite Mort", or the "little death". This, ladies and gentlemen, is called an orgasm.

Touch me here…..

In men, the sensation of orgasm is a more general all over genital sensation. While the penis is obviously the main focus, men say to me that the sensation of orgasm can come from deep within them, resonate through their testicles or ripple out from all over their genitals. Here's a description of a male orgasm as stated in Men's Health magazine in learning to be multiply orgasmic.

"Build yourself up to the brink of orgasm, then throttle back. Do this three times before climaxing. A little practice and you'll be able to feel the orgasm--racing pulse, waves of euphoria and relaxation--without ejaculating. Not only does it reduce the messy cleanup, but you'll remain erect and ready for more action." *menshealth.com*

Did you know?
That the most common time for sex is 10:30 PM according to the Durex Sex Survey

The average North American couple has sex twice a week

For female orgasm, few say it better than Mama Gena:
"Few women have felt their own true sexual pleasure erupt, like Mount Saint Helens, or crash wave after wave, like the ocean. When a woman comes like a man—all at once, like a sneeze– she limits the range of feeling possible for her by virtue of her unique physiology. Men's sexuality is goal driven, rather than pleasure driven. Women need to get in touch with the undulating, ever expanding, pulsating world of female orgasm, and to come as only a woman can _ an experience not to be missed! What most women need is an owner's manual for their very own sexual equipment." (Regena Thomashauer, *Mama Gena's School of Womanly Arts*, page 78)

Anatomy 101

Here is an understanding of all the important parts. These are the key places to touch when we are trying to stimulate to the point of orgasm. I have heard of men climaxing without touch, (they were incredibly turned on), but most need the friction of touch on one of the following parts in order to get off.

Him:

The Penis - The most sensitive part of the penis is the head of the penis. This is the little helmet that is rich in nerve endings. Many men quoted in the recent survey in Men's Health magazine say they love having the opening or the "eye" stimulated.

The Glans- This area is especially sensitive and is the red exposed skin where the head of the penis meets the **shaft**. For uncircumcised men, "the curve of the mushroom" comes when the foreskin is retracted and the glans are exposed. Love the rim, it is the center of pleasure for most men.

The Frenulum — On the underside of the penis where the skin of the foreskin comes together underneath the head of the penis is called the **frenulum**.

The Shaft—The shaft of the penis, is defined as everything from the head of the penis until it meets the body at it's base. The shaft is rich in nerve endings, and many men find stimulating the underside of the penis where the shaft and the testicles meet particularly sensitive.

The Testicles and Scrotum—The testes, the small balls that produce sperm are located in a sac called the scrotum. When not aroused, the testes can be exquisitely delicate, and need a light touch, but when aroused, the sac can be handled more roughly, and can be a source for much pleasure. Yum...

The Prostate—The prostate is a walnut-shaped gland inside the rectum that can be stimulated externally by pressing on the area about half way between the back of the testicles and the anus. This is known as the male "P" spot. Keep reading, there's more about the wonders of the P-spot to come.

"I don't have anything against actual penetration sex, but the manner in which it is normally gone about, men don't have a fucking clue." Paula Kamen, Her Way, page 73

The Perinium—The inch and a half between the testicles and the anus can be magic if you apply pressure about halfway along. Firm pressure can stimulate the prostate, feel amazing and help prevent premature ejaculation.

The Male ejaculation—What happens:

Once the male gets an erection—which happens from stimulation, fantasy, or even a stiff breeze in young men, the blood rushes to fill the three cigar shaped tubes called the cavernosa, similar to filling a garden hose with water. I can't tell you how many people I've spoken to during my radio shows that believe that the penis has a bone in it. This is untrue and just a popular urban

>  What most women wish guys would know is that we need oral sex, or at least lots of gentle, lubed touching, all around the CLITORIS for 15 to 20 minutes to come, the first time. After that, it's anybody's game. Vibrators help decrease the time it takes, but all on, near, or close to the clit!

myth. Men's Health magazine describes the erection alike one of those New Year's Eve noise makers. "You know the kind that's coiled up until you put it into your mouth and blow, whereupon it pops up and out?" That is a good analogy.

During ejaculation, contractions in the PC muscle (A genital muscle that runs the length of the genitals in both men and women. The PC muscle is important to know when we talk about keegal exercises and the need for control), and contractions inside the testicles cause the sperm to be expelled, mixed with some juices from the prostate and a gland called Cowpers, among others, to make up the white, viscous "loving spoonful" known as semen. This fluid is mixed together by the time it's shot out of the body through the tube known as the urethra. Ejaculation is usually teamed with the intense feeling of orgasm. However you can learn to stop the ejaculation and just hover at that orgasmic plateau.

" There is one sexual secret that multiorgasmic men have learned: to "unhitch" orgasm from ejaculation. Essentially, they've learned to take themselves to the brink of ejaculation, then stop and relax, allowing the rush of orgasm to sweep over them; then they do it again. (wouldn't you?) The patterns differ, some men have a series of "dry" orgasms, without ejaculating at all, then ejaculate explosively. Others ejaculate in a series, each time releasing an increasingly smaller amount of ejaculate. But they are always able to distinguish between the two." Men's Health. *Sex: A Man's Guide*, page 239.

Have a look at the following pictures which label all the important parts needed to discuss the male anatomy with a doctor, lover, or close personal friend. As well, there is an understanding of the vital parts of the female genitalia coming up. Hopefully, there will be a test later.

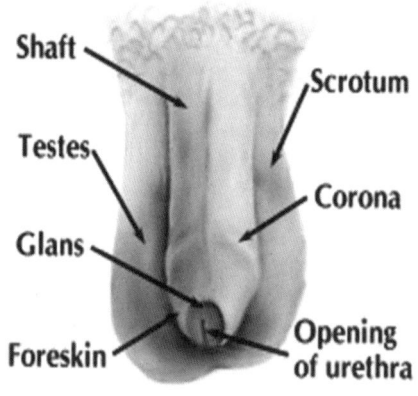

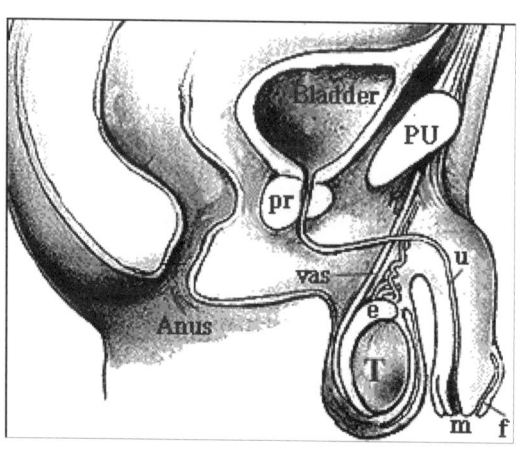

Her:

In women, the whole genital area is called the vulva. I'm reminded of the Seinfeld episode about Jerry's new girlfriend whose name he couldn't remember. He was told it rhymed with the female genitalia and he came up with the name "Mulva" (the name Doris, actually rhymed with clitoris…)

*The Kinsey study reported a high number of women who had never had an orgasm, including 25% of women in their first year of marriage.
Kinsey, 1953, page 375*

The vulva –The vulva is an area that makes up the whole female genitals. It's the whole pussy, moon of Venus, mound, or whatever you want to call it. The vulva is mainly two big areas called the inner and outer lips. These lips are known clinically as the labia minora (inner) and majora (outer). The Vulva is made up of spongy tissue that protects the rest of the delicate genital's organs. The inner lips get flushed red with blood upon arousal, and are extremely sensitive. The inner lips are sensitive, but not enough for most women to reach orgasm when stimulated. The inner lips contains some of the glands that produce sexual fluids and lubrication when stimulated.

There should be bus ads that say: WOMEN NEED CLITORAL STIMULATION TO REACH ORGASM!!!

The inner lips can often hang down longer than the outer lips, and are attached to the top of the genitals to a triangle shaped gland known as the **CLITORIS!!!!**

"Most women I interviewed mentioned a lack of information about how women achieve orgasm. When I asked specifically, information about the clitoris and G-spot was the most common answer" Paula Kamen, Her Way, page 73

There was a poll done for New Women magazine asking women if they thought their male partners knew where and what the clitoris was. The clitoris, the magic but tiny organ is the nub at the north end of the vulva. The clitoris is a large gland that's located inside the genitals with only the small tip protruding to the eye. This tip is only the top of the iceberg. The clitoral shaft is a wishbone shape with roots that extend below much of the labia minora (inner lips) In fact there are as many nerve endings in clitoris as there are in the entire penis. Hence it's VERY SENSITIVE!!!

Normally the clitoris is two to three centimeters in front of the vaginal opening, which is why less than 40% of all women are able to reach orgasm during

"The female has a greater capacity for orgasm than a man ever dreamed of " said Dr.Masters. The clitoris has no other known purpose than to provide sexual pleasure. It's women, not men, who are capable of leaping from one orgasm to the next without pausing."

intercourse, according to the Sex in America Study 1996.

Therefore, in order to reach orgasm, many women need direct clitoral stimulation, which is difficult to achieve from straight intercourse.

Most women use the clitoris to reach orgasm!

When women masturbate, most of them use their fingers or a vibrator in a circular motion on or around their clitoris. Some use the water pulsating on their clitoris from  the tap or shower massage. (The Water Pick Shower Massage– one of the best orgasmic tools around!). In fact, all women I've spoken to learned quickly about the pleasure that comes from the jetting water in a pool or hot tub. Very few women buy phallic or penis shaped dildo masturbators as sex toys. Most women can find a penis to borrow, (a willing one can be found on any street corner or bar) but what's popular are the toys that are smooth, and offer intense stimulation directly to the clitoris. Popular choices are the finger vibe and the Pocket Rocket—check the section on sex toys for more information.

"The instruction manual for a clit reads: "Educate yourself about me. Observe, listen explore, appreciate, investigate. If you love what I, the clitoris, am feeling, I will feel more, and more, and more." When women follow these simple rules, they quickly learn that the clit won't turn on when it is upset, angry, or scared. It won't be forced, or respond to abuse. If you try and rush the clit, it does not cooperate. Optimal is when the women is operating at full throttle—engorged, infused with life and enthusiasm—when she is capable of total, full-on communication, able to say "Stop it" and "More!" and everything in-between without hesitation. (Regena Thomashauer, *Mama Gena's School for Womanly Arts*, page 79)

Her parts explained:

Underneath the clitoris is the opening known as **the urethra**. The urethra is the hole where women urinate or pee from, and is significant for G-Spot orgasms as it's where the rush of fluid comes from during female ejaculation. There's a lot more about female ejaculation and the G-Spot later in this book.

All the tissue in the vulva area is made up of what's called spongy tissue. This is soft tissue, glands, with a large amount of nerve endings.

The Vagina- The vagina is a three to four inch area that has it's opening under the urethra. It's like a deflated balloon, or collapsed tunnel. The walls touch each other, but move apart to encompass anything that might enter the vaginal cavity. This is why doctors have to pry the walls apart with a speculum during examinations, in order to see the whole vagina. It's now understood that the vagina has nerve endings nicely situated near the surface that makes touching fun, and also deep pockets of nerve endings to provide resonating pleasure such as with the G-Spot orgasm. The concentration of nerve endings are near the front third of the vagina. This is not to say that the back half of the vagina has no feeling, but it is remarkably more sensitive up front. So as long as your partner has at least a three inch penis, you can be satisfied. When the woman becomes aroused, the vagina stretches to accommodate an erect penis, elongating to about four to five inches long. The vagina can also stretch widthwise, with the ability to deliver a baby with the head the size of a cantaloupe. Owww

The Vagina—X marks the spot.

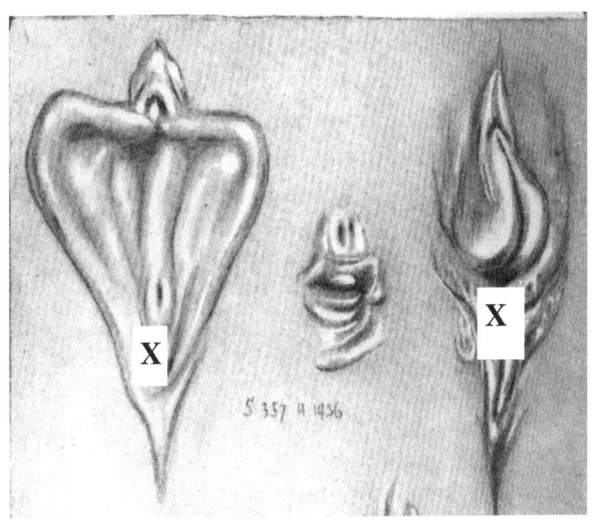

Sex with Sue tip:

Get a mirror and have a good look at your genitals. It's really hard to tell someone else about where to go, if you have no idea at all about how you're built. Check out the website

A different type of orgasm...

Repeatedly, women from all over the world have reported feeling a "different kind of orgasm" deep inside the back walls of the vagina, although the back two-thirds of the vagina has always been considered relatively insensitive. These women go on further to say that the sensations seem to contract from the inside out as opposed to clitoral stimulation which tends to be external. This type of vaginal stimulation or G-spot response often goes against traditional sexual thinking that externally is the way women want to be stimulated. For many women the stimulation of deep vaginal pressure, is what they need in order to be completely satisfied. Once the sexual revolution hit, the focus went onto the clitoris, and the chant of modern feminists has been for women to be responsible for their own orgasms.

Try using a dildo:

"Insert the dildo against the G-spot so that you feel a slight tug. Keep up the easy tugging motion as you tighten your vagina and ever so coyly tease your G-spot with rubbing. Your uterine and PC muscles will gain in strength as you tug." Barbara Keesling, Super Sexual Orgasm, page 39

Many women, and many more men, are still in the dark about female sexual responses. The wonderful British television series, *The Good Sex Guide*, told tales of the image that men had about what women wanted sexually.

"I actually started to see colors!" My boyfriend said that he never heard of anyone ever doing that, and I called him stud for a week." Leah, listener, after having a G-Spot orgasm

Many men, in their informal poll, mistakenly believed that women want 45 minutes of straight vaginal thrusting as the optimum sexual experience. What I say to listeners is that 45 minutes of straight thrusting feels like me taking the head of the penis and banging on it with your hand. It feels good for a few minutes, but after that it starts to hurt.

When in actuality what women are demanding is that their lovers be able to give them the necessary foreplay, understand the oral work of cunnilingus (female oral sex or going down), and be willing to participate in the G-spot search.

Many women believe that if their lovers can help them reach this elusive orgasm they can indeed be more receptive to regular intercourse. But a lot of men still do not have a clue about female vaginal orgasmic responses, especially, if their female partners can not help them.

The G-Spot
The G-spot is defined as a cluster of nerve endings deep in the vaginal wall, the G-spot when stimulated, can produce an incredibly intense type of orgasm.

The world of sex research has been a buzz about this new discovery, since the G-spot was first described by Bever-

Check out www.sexwithsue.com for more information and stories about the G-Spot.

ley Whipple at the annual convention of the Society for the Scientific Study of Sexuality in 1980. Many women claim that reaching a G-spot orgasm has been the high point of their sexual lives.

Women who have not experienced the type of vaginal orgasmic response a G-spot orgasm produces often feel frustrated and left out, that they are somehow missing out on a secret so special that they must be doing something wrong. I have had many women speak to me of the intense Richter scale orgasms associated with G-spot stimulation. Other women who have never heard of the G-spot and the intense orgasms it produces feel ashamed or scared when they start "gushing" and get really aroused from vaginal stimulation.

I first became interested in discussing the G-spot and disseminating information about it when I spoke to a woman who had experienced these intense orgasms and who thought something was seriously wrong with her. She had been to her doctor discussing the volumes of fluid gushing out of her, living in fear of a life threatening illness or physical deformity associated with these sensations and fluid expulsion. The later part of

Sometimes I need my boyfriend to do like he's on a construction site and jackhammer me. I need it to reach the G-spot, but only if I'm really aroused, otherwise it hurts.
Jane—29 listener

Quivering Jello: How to Have Mind-Blowing, Toe Curling Orgams has stories from real-life people who have had these kinds of orgasms and suggestions for how you can reach one too.

Unfortunately, many physicians are unaware of the recent developments in G-spot research and are unable to alleviate the fears and concerns of their patients who experience this kind of sexual stimulation. In fact, some well-intentioned but seriously uninformed doctors have even encouraged women to have surgery to correct this "problem". Producing fluid and having a mind-blowing orgasm from your vagina is not weird, or abnormal. It's healthy, sexy and something every woman should have the right to experience without shame.

Sue's tip: Play show and tell.

Nothing works better than communication. You'll just get frustrated with experimentation. Ask her directly, or suggest she show you how she masturbates.

These women thought that they were urinating, that they were incontinent. Other women have been told by their doctors to just stop having orgasms and that would stop the fluid from coming out! Obviously, these doctors weren't doing their own hands on sexual research to find out how amazing a G-Spot orgasm can be.

Sue's friend Pam says:

If you've got a flexible thumb, it's possible to reach your G-spot lying on your front with your thumb about an inch inside pressing downwards. Pam 40

27

As a sex therapist, and (for more than ten years) the host of a call-in radio talk show about sexuality, I hear all kinds of questions and problems from women and their partners about how to reach the elusive G Spot orgasm. The material collected for this book has been the result of conversations with thousands of people as a therapist and a radio host, who tried new and unique things in the bedroom. There is a collection of letters further on in this book that offer real-life suggestions and strategies couples have tried in enhancing their lovemaking.

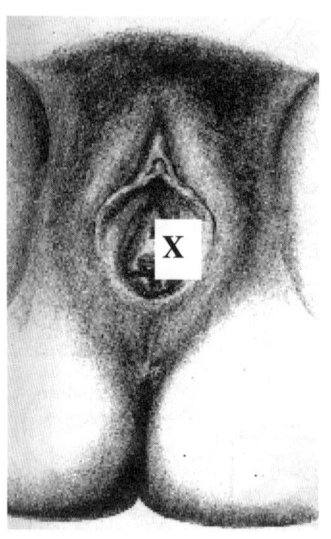

X = fingers in, north side of the vagina just past the curve of the pubic bone. Pressing down, but think of top and front. The whole area is only a few inches so your odds of reaching the G-spot are great!. Under the bladder...

In this picture, the X marks the approximate place where the G-Spot should be found. This is not the unexplored Amazon, we are talking about the whole vagina being four inches long. If you can think about the upper wall, under the urethra (tube she pees out of...) and about an inch and a half in you should at least be in the "zone".

It is an area that is often deep in the vaginal wall, and it can differ from woman to woman, but always responds to stimulation of the front wall of the vagina.

What We Know - The History of the G-spot

For many women and men the G-spot is something new, exciting and mysterious. Many people have heard of it, but still aren't clear exactly what it is. It is one of the most popular questions I get on my show, only slightly behind penis size.

In 1950, Dr Grafenberg, (hence the name G-Spot) wrote about a section of the vagina which swelled when being sexually stimulated and caused orgasmic responses. He also showed that these women could produce a clear liquid that squirted out of the glands on both sides of the urethra.

Over the past 15 years, researchers have identified certain sensitive points in the vagina. To find them, first empty your bladder, then explore with two fingers inside your vagina on the upper side; you may find it easier if you press on your stomach with your other hand. Susan Quilliam, *Every Woman's Guide to Sexual Fulfillment*. Page 171

This presentation in 1980 by John Perry and Beverly Whipple, which also showed a film to support their theories, was a great moment for women and the study of orgasms.

In this following quote by Dr. Martin Weisberg, a gynecologist from Philadelphia it illustrates why there was so much confusion about the G-Spot.

"The vulva and vagina of the person examined were normal, without anomalous or diseased nodes or places. Her partner stimulated her by inserting two fingers in the vagina and stroking along the length of the urethra. To our amazement the place began to swell up. Finally it became a firm oval about 1x2 cm, distinctly raised up above the rest of the vagina.

Shortly afterwards the person examined pressed down like having a bowel movement and just a few seconds later a milky fluid shot out of the urethra. It clearly was not urine. If the chemical analysis of the research results are right, the composition is closest to the prostatic fluid, I still cannot explain it, but I can bear witness to the fact that the Grafenberg spot and a female ejaculation exist. One day the academic staff in the Medical Faculty will make fun of the fact that it was not until 1980 that the medical profession recognized that women can also have an ejaculation. It was present in every one of the 400 women examined."
(Weisberg, Martin. A on Female Ejaculation, The Journal of Sex Research, 17 (1981) 90.

Sue Says: "Really Good sex is messy sex!"

Finding the G-spot

Finding the G-spot may seem a bit complicated at first, but the entire area is only three to four inches long and there is not a lot of surface area to explore. Put a lubricated finger or two inside the vagina, use a water-based lubricant, or baby oil if it is uncomfortable, and feel as far back as you can to find the bump or beginning of the uterus, something that feels like the end of your nose.

This is called the cervix. According to the latest sex research, the cervix, and the space beyond it called the X-spot is also sensitive to pressure. (The X Spot is an expression that refers to brand new information about women's erogenous zones.) Sometimes known as a cervical orgasm, there is much discussion about the deep rooted nerve endings in the vagina causing different types of orgasms. I feel that the X spot or cervical orgasm was first written about for modern women in Debbie Tidleman's book The X Spot.

The Vagina Explored

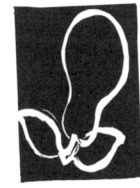

Beyond the cervix, like an upside down pear is the uterus, roughly the size of your fist, the sack in which babies are grown. If you put pressure on the front wall of the vagina, underneath the bladder, you may few the funny twinge that signals the need to urinate. It is on this front wall, roughly the size of a dime, that the G-spot exists.

This nerve center deep in the front wall of the vagina is about an inch and a half in, underneath the bladder. Don't despair initially if you poke around and do not feel anything. One listener described the amount of pressure needed, as having to press hard enough to "pick his wife up with his fingers." Very long fingers would then be needed to determine the position of the G-spot when lying on the back.

Many women I've spoken to find it easier to reach the G-spot if they "bare down" or push out with their genital muscles. Initially, the G-spot feels like a tender spot, and when the g-spot is continually stimulated then it feels like "you need to pee badly" (Carrie 27, listener) The G-spot is located just underneath the bladder, and this is a normal feeling that goes away in a moment if stimulation continues.

 The key is that if you can push through this part, and keep on continuing after short pauses, the waves of orgasm start building in intensity.

Some, but not all women if the stimulation builds (especially if there has been a recent clitoral orgasm), or if there is clitoral stimulation at the same time. My client Jennifer says it feels best

 This takes practice. It took me six weeks of trying after I first learned about the G-Spot. Don't give up.

We have this plastic bean bag chair in our bedroom. I find the reclining position and support it gives me let's my husband reach exactly the right spot. It's also easy to wipe down when I gush. Darla 32

if her partner makes a motion with her finger like a "come here" signal, that with enough pressure can bring her to a G-spot orgasm.

The Exact Spot

Let's be really clear exactly where the G-spot is. It's located roughly in the middle of the front wall of the vagina. One way to find the location of the spot is to pretend there is a clock in the vagina. If twelve o'clock is pointing to the navel, it is also indicating the position of the G-spot. The sensitive part of the spot is not exactly easy to find, being embedded deep in the vagina wall. So unlike the clitoris, this deep-seated cluster of nerve endings is not as obvious and as easy to find.

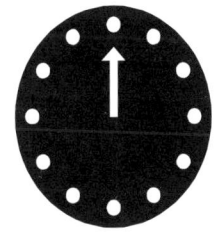

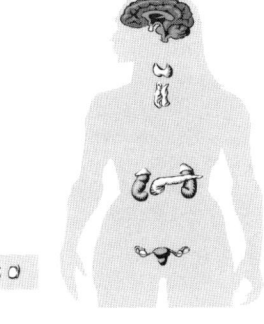

One listener suggested that if you could reach underneath the clitoris, from the inside that is where her G-spot would likely be situated.

It's all worth it....

If the G-spot is stimulated sufficiently, and the intensity is there, many women can have multiple orgasms one after the other. I had one women listener who wrote me saying she could see "colors exploding behind her closed eyes", when she was having this kind of stimulation.

Unlike clitoral stimulation, it is difficult to reach the G-spot while lying on your back with your legs apart. Lots of women connect with the G-spot by using a vibrator. The G-spot vibrator traditionally looks like the letter "J", curved at one end in order to reach this sensitive spot. The J shape puts the pressure where you need it, on this front surface of the vagina.

One of the best suggestions was one I had from a sex therapy client named Pam, who always reached a G-spot orgasm when lying on her stomach. She says her body weight helps squish everything so you can reach it. I've passed that suggestion onto a number of clients, and they found it to be a great way to start.

Www. sexwithsue.com

Here's how it's done...

One listener said she hit the biggest climax when her partner works three fingers up inside her while giving her oral sex. The key she says was having her partner say the "itsy-bitsy spider" rhyme. It kept her fingers wriggling, and her tongue right on my clit.

Your partner's co-operation is essential. You've got to be able to tell him/her what feels good, what doesn't and give instructions. So they can't feel threatened or intimidated by you saying, "A little to the left, a little to the right, a little harder, a little softer." Communication is said to be the mainstay of orgasm.

You need to be very relaxed and comfortable with your partner. You need to like your own body, really be comfortable with your own body.

You've got to just relax and be in the moment. This means you can't be fixated on your rolls of fat and cellulite, worried about stretch marks, worried about making rude noises. You don't care what your hair looks like, or that your mascara is running. You've got to be able to make noise and do what you want

 to do. Let the fluids pour out of you and let the absolute most pleasurable experience happen. It's kind of like riding a big roller coaster. Scary at first, but after it's over you want to replicate the experience immediately.
Yeah!!!!

Step 1.

Lie face down and open your legs, lifting the hips slightly. Then tell your partner to put one, or preferably two, fingers carefully into your vagina, with the palm of his/her hand downwards. He/she should  now feel in a clockwise direction round the front wall of your vagina, using a fair amount of pressure. This will move the mucous membrane to and fro. Help him/her to find the spot more easily by moving your pelvis and do not hesitate to tell them what feels good and what does not.

The first time I finally had an orgasm anywhere but with clitoral stimulation, we were trying a crazy sex position where I was resting on my shoulder doing the "riding the bike exercise". He penetrated me, while supporting his weight on the dresser. It was incredible!

If you prefer to lie on your back, your partner should insert one or two fingers in your vagina, with palm upwards. Generally they will find the G-spot by "working" the upper vagina wall with their fingers. They should do this by exerting not too timid a pressure on the point half way between the under side of the pubic bone and the end of the vagina where the cervix is located.

At the same time, your partner should place their hand on your pubic bone. In this way the G-spot is easier to stimulate.

Step 2.

Eventually you will notice the sexual excitement level rising and rising and rising and all of a sudden you will have this tremendous urge to push. It's the same sensation that women have when they're going to have a baby. They just take a deep breath and they push down right to the bottom, they just bear right down. All of a sudden this fluid literally shoots out, you do not have control. You cannot say "Ooh! I gotta stop this." You can't.

Step 3.

Lie back and think Oh my God!! I want to repeat this experience immediately! Have a cigarette if you're a smoker, and tell your partner that they are a sex God/Goddess.

Time....

The down side is that this wonderful orgasm may not happen on your first attempt But stick with it. I have found that couples who work at it consistently will find it within six weeks, I assure you the work has a big payoff.

Try this at home folks.....

Once you get the G-spot orgasm down pat, you can continue to explore the rest of the vagina and see if there are other distinct spots that can give you the same kind of stimulation. Some people feel that an orgasm-is-an-orgasm-is-an-orgasm, but I've had patients and listeners who swear that they can reach orgasms from having other parts of their bodies stimulated.

Other types of orgasms include the X spot (known as the vaginal or cervical), Urethral (stimulation of the little hole you pee out of), breast and mouth (actually reaching an orgasm from having their mouths or nipples licked and sucked), and reaching orgasm from anal sex and stimulation.

In Lou Paget's book called The Big O, she claims that women can reach different kinds of orgasms.

They are:
1. Clitoral
2. Vaginal or cervical
3. G-Spot or AFE (anterior fornix erotic) zone
4. Urethral (U Spot)
5. Breast/nipple
6. Mouth
7. Anal

In my experience, some of those listed above blur into each other, but I'll offer explanations and explore some of the sensations my patients and listeners describe the intense type of stimulation known as orgasms. Men can reach some of the same orgasms, but the big one we'll explore later on is about the P spot—or prostate stimulation. I will be going through some more detail about these types of orgasms I just listed, talking about male orgasms, and offering sexual solutions if you are having trouble getting off no matter what you try.

Trouble Shooting - Why Can't We All Reach It?

Sue says: Learn to masturbate!

So what happens if we don't reach it within six weeks of trying. What could we be doing wrong or what is holding us back? One thing could be either a lack of information about our bodies as women, or the fear of wetting the bed. Most women have been brought up traditionally, to be "good girls" and not to touch themselves or learn to masturbate. Most men however don't seem to have a problem with playing with their penises. There is an expression about male masturbation -"99% of men do it and the other 1% are lying" I firmly believe that this is a big reason why guys have a much easier time reaching orgasm. It's not the only reason, but it's a significant factor. If you aren't reaching orgasm, you need to learn to start pleasuring yourself. Think of it like exercise. You do it to keep healthy a few times a week, and masturbation is what you do to maintain sexual and orgasmic health.

Dr. Robin Baker, the leading world researcher in human reproductive functioning says that masturbation is essential for fertility and vaginal and penile health.
"First, masturbation temporarily increases the flow of mucus from the cervix into the vagina. Mucus flows slowly from the cervix at all time, but orgasm speeds it up. When a woman climaxes, the glands at the top of her cervix increase their rate of mucus production. It lubricates the vagina, and carries with it much of the cervical debris including blocker sperm and disease organisms. This is an effective way of fighting infection. Masturbation also

increases the acidity of the cervical mucus. Bacteria cannot function properly in acidic mucus. (Robin Baker, *Sperm Wars*, page 169) For men, masturbation is biology's way of keeping the sperm fresh. According to Baker, a man's body can distinguish between masturbation and intercourse, the ejaculates produced are not identical. So for both sexes, masturbation is a vital part of keeping your equipment healthy.

As little kids it is only natural to want to explore our bodies. When we figure out that sitting on our teddy bear's in such a way produces good feelings we want to repeat the experience, often to the horror and embarrassment of our parents. If you are told NO! BAD! often enough and forcefully enough we learn to associate these feelings and actions with something dirty. We deny ourselves the essential knowledge that comes with exploring our bodies. When we are with partners, it is difficult to let go and get truly into the not very lady-like noises and expressions you may make when experiencing a powerful orgasm.

Here is a great quote about a lover's reaction to a powerful orgasm.

"WOW! Her face got all twisted and contorted when she came. She looked like Whistler's mother on a really bad acid trip. She must have had a major orgasm. Maybe I'm not so bad in bed after all...." (Goofy Foot Press, The Guide to Getting it On, 1996, Page 73)

> **In order to have any kind of orgasm, I need to clench my abdominal muscles, kind of like climbing the rope during gym class.**
>
> **Cindy age 43, listener**

This is new sexual information

Information about the G-spot, the P-spot (prostate stimulation in men which is explained if you keep reading), the importance of masturbation, and new sexual trends, all seems new, but we have the same body parts we've had since we lived in caves.

According to Edward Shorter, the head of the History of Medicine program at the University of Toronto, and the author of A History of Women's Bodies (a book about women's lives in European societies from about 1600 onwards), there was once this whole female subculture of women's special knowledge that was transmitted from generation to generation in oral tradition, and men didn't find out about it. When this female subculture finally vanished, much of its special knowledge simply vanished as well, including presumably all kinds of intimate information about the female body such as female ejaculation and orgasm.

It's now modern culture, books, movies and films that offer great new insights into the world of orgasm and sex.

In the words of Willy Russell in his screen play of Shirley Valentine....

"...Do you know when I was a girl I'd never even heard of the clitoris. No one had. In those days, everyone thought it was just a case of in out, in out, shake it all about, stars would light the sky an' the earth would tremble. Hey, the only thing that trembled for me was the headboard on the bed." (Russell, Willy. Shirley Valentine, Longman, 1991, Page 9)

Sue
If you can't play with your own equipment, you shouldn't play with someone else's.

So by now you get that you need to masturbate to become incredibly orgasmic. The truth is, that some of your most powerful climaxes will be by yourself. Mama Gena explains the benefits of self pleasuring. "Taking control of your body and your pleasure is no small shakes. We're taught to sit back and let someone else drive. The truth is that if you think someone outside you controls your pleasure, you feel out of control. You can't own what you think someone else possesses or gives you. Unless you own your sensuality, you will only be dependent or needy or desperate in your couplings. True partnership comes only after true ownership." (Regena Thomashauer, *Mama Gena's School of Womanly Arts*, page 75)

So now that we know that self pleasuring is an important skill on your way to serious orgasms, lets learn about the tools and tips we need to get there.

Hallelujah!!

Keegal Exercises and the PC muscle

Orgasm from lovemaking builds intimacy. Orgasm has a relationship bonding power. After orgasms men and women feel closer to their partners, a feeling that has in part a physical basis. The chemical oxytocin, released by the brain upon orgasm has been nicknamed the "cuddling hormone" which inspires feelings of attachment.
Drs Joel Block and Susan Crain Bakos

A vaginal, G-spot or X spot orgasm is sometimes referred to as the orgasm of orgasms. Freud thought only a vaginal orgasm was a mature orgasm, but I think he still had a thing or two to learn about women's sexuality. I think an orgasm is an orgasm is an orgasm. The more the better, and who cares how you get them as long as they are good.

That being said, the internal vaginal orgasm and the Prostate stimulation (or P spot orgasm) are different than straight play with the penis or the clitoris.

It seems to come from somewhere deep inside and is a whole different sensation.

The information is that the PC muscle which runs through the genitals plays a large part in producing this internal orgasm in both men and women.

The PC muscle, runs from front to back and it supports the genitals and the anus. You can feel it under the skin about two centimeters below the spongy tissue of the vulva or the male abdomen where the penis attaches to the body. The PC muscle is stimulated by something called the pudendal nerves, which is like the sexual tuning fork. It picks up all the vibrations and action going on in the genitals, signals the brain that the orgasm is coming….(oh I'm coming….) , and is responsible for all the fun rhythmic contractions during orgasm.

Stronger!

By making this PC muscle stronger it pays big dividends for your sex life for both men and women. In most people however, this muscle is pretty wimpy. I often ask people about riding a horse or a bike for the first time in awhile, and how uncomfortable your inner thighs feel when you sit down. Muscles you didn't even know you had hurt. This is the PC muscle, one of the typically flabbiest muscles in the body.

There's a lot of guys who don't even know where the clitoris is. It just seems like they are all over the place! Even if they find the right place and you say oh yeah, they keep moving. And you're like, "no go back!"
Catherine What Women Want

However, if you can learn to strengthen it, you can be magic in the bedroom, and your orgasmic capacity will go through the roof. So how do you get hard rippling PC muscles and move into orgasmic bliss? You work 'em baby!

Two more, and squeeze…...

Dr Keegal, an observant doctor a number of years ago noticed that many women had vaginal problems after childbirth. The vagina got all stretched out of shape and many women had urine leaking problems after their first children were born. He started having his patients try an exercise that helped tremendously named, oh so aptly, Keegal exercises.

Now Keegals are great for both men and women. For women it strengthen the floor of the vagina—prevents the need for adult diapers (in both sexes as you age), causes you to have incredible inner control, and greatly increases the blood flow to the genitals, increasing the power of your orgasms.

For guys, it increases the power of your orgasms, increases the strength of your erection, and helps you last longer by "holding back" the ejaculate. This is one of the big steps needed to control your ejaculation and become multiply orgasmic. Try using the insights I just mentioned about masturbation, and try holding back while you self pleasure. You can try different sensations, masturbate with a condom on, a leather glove, anything that mixes up and changes your ejaculation.

Interesting fact:

It is rumored that Cleopatra, a few thousand years ago, had PC muscles of steel. It seems she had mastered those inner muscles, - and with them the Roman Emperors Caesar and Mark Anthony.

I do them at stop lights…..

Here's the drill. Put this book down and go to the washroom.

As you are peeing, stop and start the flow of urine. It's the muscles that allow you to stop and start that you want to target. Remember how you did that and as you read this book clench and unclench those muscles. Squeeze and release. You got it…

There are lots more detailed information on my website www.sexwithsue.com

It may not feel like you are doing anything for awhile, but keep at it, you want to get to about 100 repetitions a day. I have a sticker on the dashboard of my car that reminds me to keegal while I'm driving. During traffic lights, I try to hold my muscles tight as long as I can. You can also try little flutters of the muscle by pretending that you are an elevator. Imagine that the first squeeze is the ground floor, the next the second, and so on until you have a funny look on your face and have hit the penthouse.

I have seen women in a few adult movies and in strip clubs who have mastered these exercises. One women could pick up quarters off the edge of the table with her vagina. I've had friends who swear they've seen women who can toss ping pong balls, smoke cigarettes and play the harmonica with their

vaginas. For guys or men who suffer from pre-mature ejaculation, it's an absolutely imperative exercise. It may take you a few weeks to notice a difference—just like working out any other muscle, but your sex life will be better for it. The nice thing about keegals is that you can do them anytime and anywhere, and nobody notices.

The final benefit about keegals is that doing them increases the blood flow and can often get you aroused. If you get into the gold medal round of keegaling, you can actually bring yourself to orgasm without touching yourself. Now that should be an Olympic sport!

Keegals are extremely important. The strength of that muscle, the pubococcygeus or PC muscle, is positively correlated with a person's orgasmic response. That is, people who have weak or no orgasms, have very weak PC muscles. In women who have orgasm from clitoral stimulation, the muscle is stronger, but not as strong as women who can have an orgasm from vaginal or other types of stimulation. This muscle goes from the pubic bone to the front of the coccyx or tailbone. In animals, that muscle wags the tail. We don't have tails to wag, so the only time we use that muscle is for orgasm or to stop and start the flow of urine. Dr. Beverly Whipple, *What Women Want* page 260

Female Ejaculation from the G-Spot

Almost all men and somewhere under 40% of women can ejaculate. For men it's called the "Loving Spoonful" or about a tablespoon of white goo. This goo has about 40 calories, and becomes liquid when warmed. It also has anywhere from 150 to 300 million sperm cells for each ejaculate. The prostate makes up much of the fluid, and it contains, sugars and other "basic" or non-acidic liquid for the sperm to live safely in for three to five days inside a human body. For women, the ejaculate is sweet, clear, liquid virtually identical to the prostate fluid that makes up the bulk of the male ejaculate.

What is this liquid and where does it come from?

Today, many sexologists, feel that the G-Spot is the female equivalent of the male prostate. The prostate I explained earlier, is the gland that produces much of the semen. Known as the "P spot", because it is incredibly pleasurable if you stimulate it GENTLY, once the man is aroused. This is different than the "moon river exam"  that guys over 40 get from the proctologist or doctor that involves bending over, a rubber glove, lube and the singing of "moon river".

It's the prostate that produces most of the fluid for men, and it seems that the G-spot is the female prostate.. Biologically, all babies start out as female, and it's only the introduction of the male hormones that changes the baby male. So it seems that both sexes have a lot of the same tissue. The clitoris is the female penis, and men have nipples, even though they don't need them for lactation. Cool huh?

So in summary, today's modern sexologists believe that there is a G-spot, it can produce a "different", but powerful orgasm when stimulated, and some, though not all women can ejaculate a clover smelling fluid upon orgasm.

It's been estimated that only between 10 and 40% of women can ejaculate. There hasn't been sufficient research to control which women do and don't, but the fluid seems to be stored in something called the vaginal sponge -- a collection of fluid holding cells near the bladder. Just like your arm can swell up to huge proportions when injured, the vaginal sponge has a great capacity to hold fluid. The amount of female ejaculate or G-Spot fluid has been described as a sprinkle to a liter (or milk-bag full).

For some as yet unknown reason, not all women seem to produce this ejaculation fluid. If all women have these glands, then why don't we all ejaculate when we climax, like men do? Researchers speculate that the amount of fluid varies, as it does in men, and may at times be so small as to not be noticed, or may be confused with other vaginal secretions that occur during arousal.

Whether you ejaculate or not doesn't really matter however, since the G-Spot experience is about intense orgasmic sensations, not about producing enough fluid to soak the bed sheets. This is when you need to get out your snorkle equipment, and dive right in.

But what about the mess?

As I have already stated, not everyone ejaculates. But those who do, often ejaculate amazing amounts of fluid. If you happen to be one of those women you have to make preparations before you start.

Everybody who either peed the bed as a child, or had a child who peed. the bed knows that urine stains the mattress: you get a big, ugly, yellow ring. Then you get another ring, and eventually you have to throw the mattress out. The good news is that ejaculate is NOT urine, it does not stain the bed. It does not stain sheets. There is no odor. You can tell that it is not urine.

It's a myth that a man can't have an ejaculation or orgasm without an erection. Called soft orgasms, they are common among men with erection problems.

The only problem is, it takes a long time for it to dry on an ordinary mattress, sofa, or carpet, because the fluid soaks in. So you have to take control in advance. You can decide how you are going to handle the situation. Why not do it on his side of the bed? Let him have the wet
spot for a change. Either that or make some alternate arrangements in advance. For ex-

ample, take a big green garbage bag and open it up on one side and across the top and stretch it out, and then take a big beach-towel or a big flannelette sheet and pin the four corners to the green garbage bag. Keep that rolled up under the bed, and when you want to make love just haul it out. Then you are free to relax and forget about the mess.

Here is a letter form a listener who reaches a "gushy" G-spot orgasm, and her suggestions on how to reach it.

Dear Sue,

I am almost 30 years old and did not experience my first orgasm until I was 28! Since my first one I have talked non-stop to all my girlfriends about this and they are of the opinion that it can't possibly be as incredibly mind blowing as I say it is! Yes, you guessed it - not one of them has had the pleasure of experiencing one. I tell my partner that I think every guy should be able to come like that just once in their lifetime just so they can experience what a rush it is! I had difficulties climaxing clitorally, but much more easily hit a deep vaginal G-spot orgasm. I still climax best from fingers deep inside me. I'm the queen of female ejaculation.

My first orgasm happened in the summer of 1997 and I was lying on my back and he was above me on his knees. The partner I was with at the time had apparently been with a lot of women that had experienced orgasms before. When I came, all he could say was "look what you're doing to my bed - oh my God - stop it!" Needless to say, I was hurt by his words but at the same time I had a smile on my face because it was such a great feeling.

The lover I have now, whom I've been with for just over a year, truly enjoys giving me orgasms as much as I enjoy having them! Every time I have one he still can't believe the amount of liquid that comes out—sometimes neither can I! The only disadvantage to having such large orgasms is that I've ruined my couch, and my brand new bed is almost written off too. (It's a good thing my lover knows someone who works at Sleep Country Mattresses!!)

Jessica 29 listener

"Sometimes when I'm close and he knows that, he just stops. I hate it. Guys do it to make it last, savor being on the brink. The difference is that guys can always come. Women can't. Christina Men's Health

Therefore, since it is difficult, if not impossible to produce this G-spot orgasm and ejaculate by oneself it is no wonder that most women haven't experienced it. The women who manage it without a co-operative partner are able to put pressure on their bladder on the lower abdomen, or are very proficient with the G-spot vibrator in order to reach this orgasm.

> There are more of these helpful comments on my website at www.sexwithsue.com

Problems reaching orgasms

Him:

Believe it or not, there are lots of men that experience difficulties reaching orgasm. They fall into two categories; either retarded ejaculation—which is difficulty ejaculating any and all the time, or just having difficulty orgasming from intercourse or other sexual positions such as oral sex.

Guys who can't seem to ejaculate or have the sensations of climax usually have a physical problem. Like with erection problems, ejaculation problems are not all in your head.

Hormonal problems—It's not unheard of for guys to have a testosterone or progesterone imbalance related to both orgasm difficulties, and low sex drive.

Solution:
The nice thing about hormonal problems is that they are relatively easy to test for (see your doctor for a blood test), and the medication can be simple and effective. The problem is there are often side effects, and one size treatment doesn't fit all, but see an endocrinologist (hormone doctor) if you think this may be the problem. The testosterone patch, (like the one they use for menopause and for stoping smoking) can deliver a regular dose of sex drive hormone.  It turns out that lesions on the pituitary gland for both men and women can lead to an inability to reach orgasm. These lesions are successfully treated surgically.

Prostate problems-
This is the biggy. The saying is that every guy, at one point or another will have prostate trouble.  Marks the spot! Urologists, (penis doctors) don't seem to know why the prostate enlarges, it just does. It's a big problem for men in their 50's, but even younger men suffer from it. The prostate is like a donut circling the urethra tube that brings urine and ejaculate out of the body. The prostate starts to squeeze, and nothing is getting through that sucker but a dribble—forget the explosion.

"**Although not as many men develop prostate cancer as prostate enlargement, it has become the most common cancer in humanity, and gram for gram, more trouble occurs in the prostate gland, than in anywhere else in the male body.**" Yosh Taguchi –<u>Private Parts</u>, page 57

Solution:
This is a medical problem. While there are some herbs you can take, to try and reduce the prostate inflammation, medical treatment is something you need to get (see above quote if you need any incentive)

If you feel like you are sitting on a stone, have that burning sensation when you urinate or ejaculate. Or if you are having the drips, either with urine or with semen, then it's time to see your doctor for an appointment with a rubber glove…..

King Louis XVI of France couldn't have sex with Marie Antoinette. It turns out that he had an excessively tight foreskin and needed a circumcision. He went on to have two children.

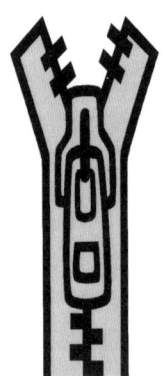

Sensation Problems—One of the more common problems I see from men as a sex therapist, especially if they have been single for awhile, is difficulty orgasming from intercourse. The truth is that you get a lot more sensation from the hand or from oral sex than you do from the vagina. The vagina may be loose, and not have enough friction to reach orgasm. The other problem is that sex is about habits, and men have both erection and ejaculation problems when they try new things on a penis used to the same old stimulation. As an example, the penis used to masturbation can think intercourse is ho hum, and need a quick hand job to climax.

Solution:

This problem has a great deal to do with your head. Relaxing and realizing that this is a common problem might help,

You also have to train your penis to like different types of stimulation. Try getting your partner to use some of those cool new love sleeves, or try using a terry cloth, leather, or try a fabric glove when you play with yourself. Some of those new massage sleeves are supposed to feel "crazy" on the glands at the head of the penis. You might also want to try bringing yourself to the brink of orgasm with a good bout of oral sex or masturbation, then insert quickly into the vagina to finish off. It's all about practice and conditioning your penis. With a little help from a friend you should be howling at the moon in no time!

Her Orgasm Troubleshooting Problems:

Never experienced an orgasm:
The research is that over 10% of women (closer to 20% of women under 21) have never, ever reached an orgasm.

Many of the problems relate to a lack of understanding of what kind of stimulation works for you, and the rest has to do with specific problems that I'll address here.

"If you reach the plateau, move your body around as if you are having an orgasm. Exaggerate the pretend orgasm. Act as if it were very intense. Make a lot of sounds, and you could be surprised by a real one!
Lonnie Barbach, For Yourself

Hooded Clitoris:
One of the explanations about why women have difficulties reaching orgasms is that they may have extra flesh covering the hood of their clitoris. The covered hood means you need direct stimulation, and lots of it.

Solution:
A big help is intense focused sex toy vibrators like the Pocket Rocket or the Silver Bullet (see section on sex toys for more information). You might want to look into some of the recent literature about clitoral hood piercing as a suggestion to try. I know it sounds scary (and hey, who am I to talk, I don't even have my ears pierced), but the women I've spoken to say it really works. The nub of

the ring rubs against the clitoral shaft and can cause orgasms going up stairs. You can always remove the ring if you don't like it!

Too Intense:

I hear a lot of women tell me that if they are having oral sex or getting manually stimulated (fingered), they feel the sensations getting too intense. They find that they have to have their partner stop, they get close but the feelings are just too much. That's where the frustration comes in.

A recent trend for all women having difficulties reaching orgasm is to consider a clitoral hood piercing. The ring rubs against the clitoris that can make even climbing stairs an orgasmic experience!

If you could watch most women masturbate, you would find that many of them stop the stimulation for 20 seconds or so, and them resume. They may have to do this eight or nine times until the orgasm comes in a rush. Orgasms are like bicycles: once you learn to reach one, you never forget!

"As soon as I begin rubbing my clitoris I get a pleasant ticklish feeling, and whenever I hit an especially sensitive spot, my whole body jerks slightly. After ten minutes of rubbing, a new sensation takes over, and I know I am about to have an orgasm."

Lonnie Barbach, For Yourself, page 72

Another problem is where to stimulate:

Most women (unless you have extra flesh) find stimulating right on the clitoris too intense.

Unless it comes from oral sex where the rule of thumb is to find the clitoris and don't move, vibration or fingers should be to one side or the other of the clitoral shaft.

The best way to solve this problem (after masturbating and learning about yourself) is to communicate what feels good to your partner. Try practicing in the mirror if you are too shy to tell your partner. When you can say it effortlessly, without being defensive (kind of matter-of-fact) then you are ready.

Vulva Pain

Many women suffer from soft tissue pain in and around the vulva. It's often red and swollen, and hurts like crazy when touched. This doesn't lend itself well to intense stimulation, and mind-blowing orgasms. Usually, the problem is related to something called vulvodynia—which means, essentially vulva pain. This is very real and needs to be treated medically.

More recent research has shown that vulva pain may be linked to cystitis—which is an infection and inflammation of the urethra (the tube you pee out of!). This is related to bladder infections, and too much rough sex. There is something called Honeymoon cystitis, which you get from having too much sex in a short period of time.

Deep Vaginal Pain:

When it comes to intercourse, many women experience a deep vaginal pain. Your doctor can eliminate the obvious problems, sexually transmitted diseases, infections, blocked gland. Go to the doctor, and get any basic problems ruled out. If the doctor can't find anything, and you are still experiencing these problems here's what you should consider. In my experience there are basically four common problems that are not immediately obvious.

1. **Painful intercourse with a sore cervix.** Some guys, especially those who are well-endowed can bang on the back of the cervix (remember, it feels like the end of your nose) during intercourse. The cervix causes a jarring of the ovaries (like super-sensitive testicles) and you hurt. Time to tell him to stop sinking it to the nuts if he wants to continue having sex with you. Being on top should also help. You can get a "door stop" or donut to block him (so you don't feel him knocking at the back of your throat!)

2. **Endometriosis**
Endometriosis is when your menstrual blood goes up instead of down, and attaches to your internal organs. It looks like bits of dark blood attached all over your internal organs. It hurts (big ouch) and has to be lasered off. Go see your doctor and get it treated—the sex will be much improved.

Vaginismus
Vaginismus is the painful spasm of the vaginal muscle. For women who have been abused, or are super nervous or uptight about sex, the vaginal muscles tighten and cramp. Kind of like the

The reason self stimulation works so well to produce orgasm is that you are the only one involved. You can focus totally on yourself, take as much time as you need, and you don't need a partner who is willing to cooperate.

> The power of a man's tongue on his lover cannot be underestimated-this warm, wet sensation can levitate most women. As one woman said, "There is nothing that compares to his mouth. It is softer, warmer, and he does much more with it." Tongue motions include circular with the taste bud surface, up and down or back and forth with a broad tongue surface. The combination of moves can create an endless variety of pleasure, but it's always best to start soft and build sensation gradually. *Lou Paget, <u>The Big O</u>, page 82*

headaches and stiff neck you can get when you're tense, some women hold their tension in their PC muscles. Keegals help, so does lots of gentle foreplay and a relaxed partner. This is what's going on when you hear of people actually being stuck together during sex. This is something you might need to see a sex therapist to treat.

G-spot pain

Since I've explained that the G-spot is essentially a female prostate (and the prostate is a male G-spot or P spot), problems that affect the prostate can also affect the tissue around and making up the G-spot. For example, new tests have been developed to test for prostate problems, similar to the tests conducted on men to evaluate for cancer. Lots of doctors haven't heard of it, so if you continue to be frustrated by mysterious vaginal pain, mention that you may have prostatitis.

Some of the latest research suggests that a small percentage of women may have spinal cord abnormalities, or "wiring" problems such as diabetic neuropathy, multiple sclerosis, or other neurological problems. These are serious on their own and may cause sexual dysfunction and inorgasmia (inability to reach orgasm). Unfortunately, these medical problems are harder to treat, but Lonnie Barbach's book <u>For Yourself</u> offers step by step orgasm training that you may be helpful.

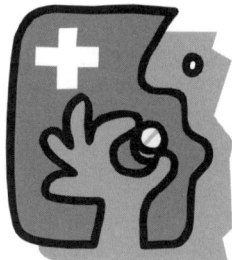

The last suggestion that comes out of the current research on inorgasmia, suggests that drugs like antihistimine, can affect orgasmic response. It may open your sinuses, but close down the pleasure centers in the brain.

Finally if you have never had an orgasm don't give up. We are all built for pleasure, and I think it's a God-given right. Get a physical, a blood test to check your hormone levels, and spend some time with yourself and one of the following sex toys that are exceptionally good at finding the sweet spot and turning you into quivering jello.

Spanish Fly or cantharides, is made by crushing a dried poisonious meloid beetle found in Mexico and the Mediterranean. While having some of this dried beetle causes a warming and irritation to the genitals, a mere one thousandth of an ounce is enough to destroy the kidneys. Spanish Fly is considered a class 1 poison, and is banned in North America.

 Sue's Tickle Trunk…..

SEX TOYS….

My favorite sex toys, that will make you stiff necked in no time!

 Here's the list of the best, most reasonably priced sex toys that will bring you to an orgasm. Most of them focus on women, but for guys, the new jelly sleeves are the thing to buy. There's a new one called Senso lips that's supposed to be incredible! Get more information and reviews on my website **www.sexwithsue.com**. Having a better and more powerful orgasm can get easier if you have the right technology. The truth is that we do get our most powerful climax when we are alone. The joys of self love or masturbation should not be underestimated. Nobody

 can read minds, and can offer the instant feedback you can give yourself. It doesn't replace a partner, but it does give you the information and technique to know what your body is capable of in respect to the quivering jello quotient.

All these sex toys get my Blue Ribbon Rating!

The Hitachi Magic Wand

A plug-in toy with a foot-long handle and a heavy duty rounded head. The Magic Wand has for years been the yardstick by which all other toys are measured. Considered the essential toy for anybody looking for serious power, the Magic Wand allows you to reach that muscle that is aching and throbbing so much, or even to use it on sore muscles other than the ones between your legs. The Magic Wand is a plug-in toy so you don't have to worry about your batteries dying during a critical moment. It will bring orgasm after orgasm, even if you've had difficulty in the past. The Magic Wand is a long-life investment, and well worth every penny. This is an award winning vibrator!

Finger Vibe

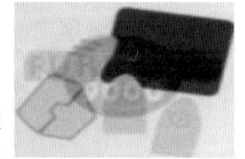

The product of the year in the adult toy world, this small, incredibly powerful vibrator fits easily on your finger so that you can apply it exactly where you need it. Great for women who have difficulties reaching orgasm or are new to sex toys. Simply place the soft micro vibrator on your finger and adjust the variable speed as required. It's also terrific for male partners, as the flexible fingertip works like your own hand to offer a new type of stimulation to the penis shaft, testicles and anus. Finally, you can reach the world of orgasmic bliss quickly and consistently. And it's right at your fingertips.

The Tongue

Many rate this life-like, soft and flexible tongue the #1 sex toy available.

Considered by Playboy to be one of the most orgasmic and successful erotic toys ever made. Redbook magazine calls it the #1 sex toy in the world and noted that it is designed and made by a woman who understood what women really wanted from a bedroom toy after conducting exhaustive research. The Tongue is a life-like, soft and flexible toy of amazing strength that looks like a large tongue. Different from other toys in that it doesn't vibrate, it actually moves like a tongue, undulating back and forth to give you an unbelievable sensation that is unique to The Tongue. It goes from slow to Ohhhhhh in one flick. The Tongue can be used either with batteries or with any regular adapter for never fail use. The five speeds can build to a ferocious pace with a never tiring, never changing massage and rhythm. For any woman with a preference for straight up oral stimulation, The Tongue is magic with a little lube, and is great for ensuring strong, consistent orgasms.

Tickling Panties
These are panties that have a secret. The small vibration pouch (which can be

whisper quiet), powerful vibrations and small hideaway variable speed control lets you experience the ultimate in orgasmic satisfaction anywhere you desire These panties give a whole new meaning to the word housework. No one will know it as you bliss out all day in total rapture. Mix business with pleasure, or heighten the pleasure of your mixing.

Tickling Bra
If you are one of the many who can't get enough attention to your breasts, then the Tickling Bra is for you.

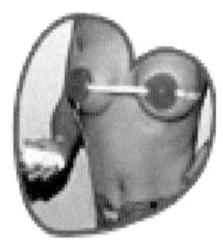

It's a fact that some women go absolutely wild for nipple stimulation. Think of it as little vibrators pressed into flat pads that are concealed in your bra, with adjustable, removable straps for comfortable, invisible support. It has a sucking motion and is quiet, turning a padded bra into your best friend. For any woman who turns to Jell-O with nipple play, there is no other product like the Tickling Bra to put you in charge of the type, amount and speed of stimulation, anytime and anywhere.

Cybersleeve
A silicone jelly snug sleeve that feels like hundreds of tiny fingers are caressing your penis.

This item is acclaimed as the second wonder of the world among men I've spoken to. With a little lube it's guaranteed to make you wonder why you haven't tried it before. Think of a moist, tight sheath of soft, pulsating, incredible lifelike jelly.

Passion Pearl
The Passion Pearl hits all the right spots at the same time with both a strong penetrative penis-shaped shaft and a soft clitoral-tickling device.

This is similar in design to the dragon, bunny or any of the more popular Asian toys. When both features are used together, Quivering Jello you shall be! But this jelly vibrator comes with state-of-the-art controls and instant reverse so that you can also enjoy the sensations of each feature individually as well as together, while having full control over each. This is a personal favorite and one of the best selling all-purpose toys ever made.

Silver Bullets
A small, silver love bullet with attachments which can be used inside and out.

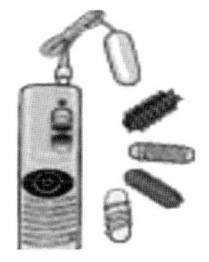

These items deliver incredible torque for their size. They are small enough for internal use, and the rounded end is gentle against nipples, testicles and the head of the penis. They are discreet enough to hide in the bottom of your purse, and so innocent looking that it won't cause your mother to raise her eyebrows if she happens to look in your bedside table. The bullets, which can be used inside and out and be put into two places at once are a must first toy to have for any couple starting to experiment with creative sex play.

The Pocket Rocket

A great little toy that really moves, the Pocket Rocket has been around for awhile and is always in the top 5 most popular toys. Small enough to fit into a lipstick case, the pocket rocket doesn't look like a sex toy. The little balls offer stimulation just where you want it and nowhere else. A great little toy, and the first one I recommend for women having difficulties reaching jello-like orgasms.

> In Lou Paget's book, The Big O, Lou recommends using a thirty-six inch strand of costume pearls as a sex toy. "Lubricate his penis, then slowly adorn him by wrapping the pearls around the shaft. Be sure to hold the necklace clasp with one finger, as you don't want it to scratch and distract him. If you've worn them out for dinner, the pearls will be softly warm. When his penis is wrapped in pearls, then start stroking him up and down with a gentle twisting motion. You can then unwrap his penis and, almost like you are flossing under his testicles, slowly pull the pearls from one side to another, slightly lifting his testicles. And when you are done you can "coil the poiles" at the base of his shaft and settle yourself on top of him. (Lou paget, The Big O, page 198-199)

Wall-Socket Sex!

How to take your orgasms into the wow zone!

The rest of *Quivering Jello: How to have Amazing Orgasms that will turn you to Mush!* will focus on suggestions for taking your orgasm from thank-you-very-much, to Oh-my-God,- I-love you , and you are a sex God/Goddess! I will also offer up suggestions for finding those hard to reach orgasms like the P and X spots, and letters written by real women reaching real orgasms. I can give you all kinds of suggestions, but hearing about how real people climax, and how they do it specifically may put you over the edge.

Interesting Fact:

Catherine the Great of Russia was known for her sexual adventures. She used to get lovers out of huge military and tie silk scarves around the top of their testicles. These scarves prevented the testicles from moving up against the body, which is what happens to all men before they ejaculate. These scarves were tight and helped her lovers keep going all night.

X marks the spot

Debbie Tidleman wrote a book called the X spot detailing how women can reach amazing orgasms by stimulating right on the end of the clitoris.

Other books have since been written about the spot. There was a book called *The Super Sexual Orgasm* by Dr. Barbara Keesling which called it a Cul de Sac orgasm, and an explanation about vaginal cervical orgasms are written in Lou Paget's book, *The Big O*.

Dr. Keesling writes "the key to the super sexual orgasm lies within a small passage of the vaginal canal, just beyond the cervix, known as the cul-de-sac. This small section of the vaginal canal is so extraordinarily enriched in sensitive nerve endings that in some women the slightest contact with a man's penis or sex toy can trigger instantaneous orgasm." (page 62)

I know a number of women who can reach incredible "wall socket" orgasms by having the back of their vagina stimulated. Go in feel for the cervix or the small hole that is the opening of the uterus, and apply firm pressure to the area. Debbie Tidleman describes it as going all the way to the back, and then pulling forward ever so slightly.

Here are two letters from listeners that describe reaching the X and G spot.

Dear Sue,

I can honestly say I have never had a lover like Joe. While I have a healthy attitude towards sex and have had other men, I can see now I was only having sex. From the first night Joe and I made love, it just keeps getting better.

I had heard about the G-spot but never knew where and what it really was. One night while Joe and I were having foreplay (which, I may add, can last up to one hour), I had a wild thing happen. He had his finger in my vagina and I had the sensation that I was peeing while I was having the most incredible orgasm. At first I was embarrassed but he told me that I was not peeing but had gushed all over his hand. We thought this may have been a G-Spot thing and we looked up the information on your web site (www.sexwithsue.com) and yes, I had a classic G-Spot orgasm.

More real-life, honest-to-goodness orgasm letters on my website www.sexwithsue.com

I was very curious, so one evening he set me up on some pillows got a mirror and a light and gave me a tour of my genitals. With his finger over mine, he helped me find my G-spot which seem to be an inch in on the top of the vagina wall. He helped me to orgasm and we both had very wet fingers. I can also have one when we use the position with me lying on my tummy and him entering from behind. The whole experience is so hot.
Jamie—listener

Dear Sue,

My partner and I have been together now for 20 months and the sex is getting better and better every time we make love. She cannot reach orgasm by penetration alone, but we found a way. As I am penetrating her, she stimulates her clitoris with her fingers, and can come that way very easily. But the best orgasm she enjoys is, when I am going down on her and at the same time inserting two fingers and stimulating her deep inside. It almost feel like I'm fisting her with half my hand up her vagina. It's tight, but the visual sure turns me on. She always reaches her orgasm with a big O, and lots of screaming. Since we

live in an apartment, and her scream is very loud, I have to close the windows before we make love, even on a very hot day), and her face plus her upper body become very red and hot to the touch. I feel very good after I make her come and the best part is, after that, she will give me the best oral sex of my dreams, every time...

Jeff—listener 33

The P spot and stimulating the male parts...

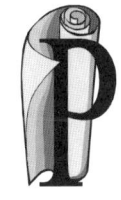

The truth is that most guys love anal stimulation. The male anus and rectum is chocked full of nerve endings, and you have the added benefit of the prostate gland which is super sensitive. If guys can get away from the gay thing they realize that anal stimulation opens up a whole new area to explore and get turned on by. In fact rectal stimulation is one of the top ten most common male sex fantasies according to phone sex surveys. (the top three are sex with two women, having anal sex, and light S & M bondage). You can stimulate the P-spot in a variety of ways, but the easiest and most direct involves gentle finger stimulation.

1. If you go half way between the back of the testicles and the anus and press firmly, while offering the penis some encouragement at the same time, you should hit the prostate.
2. By inserting your clean finger (watch out for the nails!) into the rectum you can feel for the spongy, round gland of the prostate. If you move it back and forth, again while rubbing or sucking the penis your partner should start singing Ava Maria.

Stop and Start

Beyond strengthening your PC muscles by doing your keegal exercises and keeping your testicles from moving up against the male body to prevent ejaculation, there are two other techniques guys can use to prolong the orgasm and delay ejaculation.
Try some P spot or perinium stimulation when the man is close to ejaculating as described in the previous para-

graph. Pressing down on your perinium (to hold back ejaculation) can not only feel great but help separate the sensations of orgasm and ejaculation. The other technique is called the stop start technique and is very effective for delaying ejaculation. *Sex, A Man's Guide* describes it like this.

Find out more with letters from guys who've experienced multiple orgasms at www.sexwithsue.com

"Basically, you simply masturbate to the brink of ejaculation, then stop; do it again, then stop until your body learns to gain control over what is wrongly perceived as one of the most uncontrollable of impulses. Eventually, with any luck you'll begin to have the amazing experience of reaching orgasm without ejaculating." (page 241)

Some therapists recommend that you squeeze the tip of the penis tightly just before ejaculation (sometimes called the squeeze technique, but in both my practical and theoretical experience as a therapist and partner, just learning where the point of no return is will work just as well. You just need to practice, training your body in a new way and with new sensations.

The only downside is that you need to restrain yourself from "regular masturbation" or grabbing protruding parts of your body while in the shower... I promise, if you discipline yourself to gain control over your ejaculation you'll be a great lover and probably end up as a "multiply-orgasmic man".

Tantric Sex

There has been a great deal of interest in Tantric sex and the mystical benefits of spiritual connection to enhance lovemaking. Friends of mine, Pala Copeland and Al Link, run workshops called 4 freedoms Tantra, and they told me of their experiences.  They basically said that if they had extended lovemaking for prolonged periods of time, and built the sexual charge up to a certain level then touching legs, hands, or any other parts of their bodies resulted in waves of pleasure pulsing through them. Again, they've learned techniques so that the male partner doesn't ejaculate, and they spend a great deal of time everyday making love and building up their sexual charge.

"Many of us may have one memory of such an experience when sex transported us to another realm. This sometimes occurs only with one person and fleetingly, but it is experienced as a hugely different connection and state during lovemaking. Some of the masters of spiritual sexuality refer to this state as ecstasy and think of it as the supreme form of making love. For those of us who have had this experience, it seems to come out of nowhere, an event that is out of our control.
Lou Paget, *The Big O*, page 210

The workshops they run (and everything I have learned about Tantric sex) emphasize positive relationships and creative ways to enhance your lovemaking techniques. It's also about connecting with your partner. There is a lot of truth to the belief that people who are truly connected have amazing sex.

Other Types of Orgasms

Breast Orgasm
When I was nursing my son I would go to a nursing support group. I met several women there who became incredibly sexually aroused and reached orgasm by nursing their babies. The lactation consultant said that was common, especially with the new breast pumps. I agree once the pain ended about eight weeks into it, nursing was a pleasant experience, but I never came even close to reaching an orgasm. I wonder how those children were ever weaned. Apparently, some women experience breast orgasms just by playing with their nipples or by having a lover suck on their breasts. Breast stimulation triggers the release of the hormone oxytocin, which causes uterine contractions, and it's enough to bring some lucky women to orgasm.

> "Sue, my most memorable orgasm happened during Frosh week my first month at University. I was sexually inexperienced, and hooked up with this grad student who spent half the night making out with me, licking and sucking my nipples and breasts. It caused waves of heat and pleasure, and I almost collapsed."
> Mandy 28, listener

Mouth Orgasm
I once had a patient who swore that she could have mouth orgasms. Just like people who can climax through fantasy or by rubbing their thighs together, there are real, live people who can climax just by being kissed. (I'm so jealous). In Lou Paget's book, *The Big O* she describes how some men and women reach orgasm by kissing, or by giving oral sex. This was roughly the premise for Deep Throat (actually, she was to have a clitoris in her throat).

According to Dr. Herbert Otto's study, of his 205 member research group, 20% had experienced a mouth orgasm. (*The Big O*, page 109)

   Extended Sexual Orgasm

Don't forget to visit www.sexwithsue.com for more details about Extended Sexual Orgasm

Extended Sexual Orgasm or ESO is all about the kind of lovemaking that lasts hours and hours. It's basically having the kind of dirty weekend everyone hopes for where you use different positions, along with massage, oral techniques, toys and every kind of stimulation you can think of to be sexual for hours and hours. It's difficult to do for regular sex, but can make those special occasions, fun, and sexy marathons. But it's called extended sexual orgasm not just extended sex, and for that we need to start getting into multiple orgasms.

Here is what is suggested for male extended orgasm.

"Just remember, the ejaculation is not the orgasm for the man. The orgasm comes from the intense, pleasurable contractions that precede the ejaculation, and, with practice, you can cause him to have hundreds, even thousands of these contractions during a lovemaking session. Bob and Leah Schwartz, *The One Hour Orgasm*, page 142

"After your man has been stimulated for a while and has reached a fever pitch, sit astride his chest with your back to his face. Firmly grasp the root of his penis with one hand, and, with the other stroke upward very rapidly and sharply. Wait for the space of one heartbeat and repeat. Give him about ten of these and then ten more of the rapid stroke but all in quick succession with no pausing in between. Alternate these two stroking groups (one with pauses, one without) for about five to eight minutes or until he screams for mercy. Finally, give him a spectacular orgasm by way of your hand, mouth or vagina." (N. Hayden, *Overnight Orgasm*, page 82)

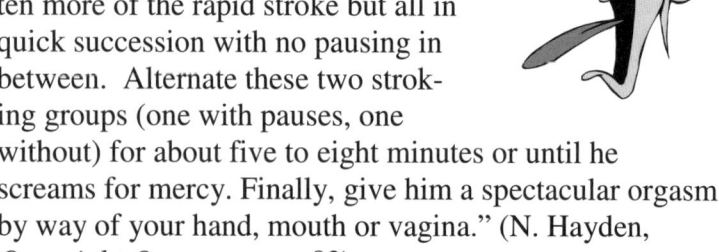

Extended sexual orgasm can be effectively experienced with G-spot orgasms. In the following letters real-life listeners offer up suggestions for reaching vaginal or G-spot orgasms.

Dear Sue,

For a full year, starting in April of last year, I had a partner who delighted in finding out all there was to know about my body and how it worked. He exhibited much of his female (sensitive) side so his natural intuition and perception were heightened (to that of many men). His success at finding out my sexual nuances left me astonished and, at times, slightly frightened. Had I been a teenager, I would never have been able to handle his discoveries and demands. As it was, I frequently was left dazed and waited anywhere from a few minutes to a full hour for my soul to catch up (do not compare this to catching your breath - it is far more awesome than that).

E-mail me your orgasm stories at www.sexwithsue.com. You can also be in my new book, *Giant Phalluses*, about penises and penis size if you send me your letters, tips, secrets, concerns or experiences with a penis you love.

My body and my willingness taught us both a great deal. I think he read articles on sexual response, especially the G-spot, and probably listened to your show (I wouldn't be surprised if he called in). Under his touch (should I call it his spell) and assisted by his voice, my body wouldn't stop. His fingers on those nerve endings resulted in multiple orgasms. In the beginning, as my body was conditioned to his touch, we would try to count the number of climaxes. Within weeks, we couldn't keep up and it was difficult to distinguish the end of one and the beginning of the next.

Whatever was beneath us - towels, a blanket folded in four, bed covers—continued, my breasts became larger than they'd ever been outside of two pregnancies.
I even changed my bra style to accommodate and accentuate a cleavage I'd never had before.

I was soaked. Once I was fully excited and had climaxed a number of times, I would squat over his belly (which he loved). All he had to say then was, "more", and I would pour all over him, as often as he requested, without him touching me. Usually it was I who had to roll away and ask him to stop. His belly and genital area would be dripping wet and he'd be enthralled with the experience.

When he knelt at my open legs, with me on my back, the stream of liquid sometimes visibly crossed the distance between my vulva and his belly. Though it often made me feel self conscious, he was fascinated by it. To me the experience was surreal and took some getting used to. I seemed to have little or no control over it.

> **Sue Says: All the really good things in life are messy!**

He would also go down on me orally and drink the sweet liquid - his tongue was as wicked as his fingers. Then he'd come back up to kiss me and let me taste the fluid - and, sure enough, it was clean and clear and totally inoffensive.

He would ask me to stand over him, hands against the wall at the head of the bed, and he would start by touching me and I would pour. Then just his voice saying, "more", and I kept going until my legs gave out. I could hear him struggling to drink my fluid - I feared I'd drown him.

Though I again was self conscious, he made me feel safe and cherished. He was as astonished by my body's reaction as I was. He absolutely loved these moments and his eyes showed awe and pride. Later he would bring me water or lemonade. I have no idea how much fluid I would lose but I'm sure it came close to a liter at times. I never seemed to run out. I wondered if I could become dehydrated - we joked about

Come Here said the "G"

how we would explain a severe case of dehydration to my doctor.

It might be safe to assume that the body's reaction is similar to that of nursing - lactating breasts fill up with a lot more milk a few days after a birth than on the first day and continue to fill to satisfy the baby's needs. Perhaps the body adjusts to keep supplying the G-spot fluid on demand.

On the subject of breasts - when liquid output was excessive, I'd sure know it the next day. My breasts would be engorged and ultra sensitive. I couldn't bear to have them touched - I could barely stand putting on a bra.

As time went by we also discovered erogenous zones we hadn't known about. A dangerous spot on him was his earlobe. He would go nuts when I sucked on it. It was fabulous! I also discovered the spot at the base of his testicles where I could feel his pulses as he climaxed. He liked me touching that area. Fact is, he reacted to my every touch. His nipples were as sensitive as his penis. His body would quiver with a touch of my fingers or tongue.

Dangerous spots on me, besides the obvious, were my big toes and index fingers. I climaxed easily when they were sucked. I once climaxed while we were driving and I was holding his hand. Our bodies knew each other so very well and the electricity was tangible.

*****Germaine—28, listener**

 This is a letter from a listener who talks about how she needed practice (got better with time), allowed herself to let go for the first time, and experience both an amazing G-spot orgasm, and the kind of orgasm where you actually see stars.

 **Don't forget, more cool stories, experiences and information on my website, www. sexwithsue. com!**

Dear Sue,

I didn't believe the G-Spot existed, well maybe I believed it did exist, but not for me. Nor was I that interested in finding out about it. However, approximately seven months ago I met a wonderful man who turned not only to be what I was looking for emotionally, but as a lover he was outstanding with no inhibitions and great interest in sexual matters. He brought up the topic of the G-spot orgasm, which I had heard of, but don't believe that I had experienced, although I did admit that I enjoyed the actual act of intercourse immensely (more than most women did as I had learned from my female friends). It felt very, very good and I now believe that it was probably because in some instances the man's penis was probably stimulating my G-spot area.

This lover of mine, who had experimented with previous partners, convinced me it was worth looking for and so our research began. And yes, he warned me that it would feel as if I had to pee and he was right. He at first

located the G-spot area using his fingers, up inside the front wall of the vagina and we knew he had found it as soon as I started complaining of the urge to urinate. We tried to keep going and overcome those feelings and sometimes it did start to feel better and quite interesting, but that was about all. But every few lovemaking sessions we would try again. He would manu-
ally stimulate the G-spot area which would at first make me feel as if I had to go to the bathroom, but he would talk me through it, and we would persevere and eventually feelings and sensations would become quite pleasant. We also discovered that if I was extremely aroused already and had already experienced a "conventional" orgasm that it was easier and felt better when the G-spot area was stimulated.

T his went on for a few months (three to four) and then it became easier and easier for me to become aroused when my lover stimulated me in this way. It would now work both manually and through intercourse with his penis stimulating my G-spot. I would start to feel a buildup of pressure. I would describe it like being engorged and it felt like something was going to happen, but I wasn't sure what. And this is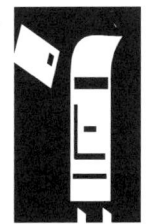
where trust and psychological understanding takes over. For although we were
in love and had an excellent sexual relationship, I think at this time I was holding back psychologically because I

was afraid of letting go and losing control. After all, this was an entirely new experience for me (imagine feeling like a virgin at 38) and fear of the unknown probably kept me from enjoying the experience as much as I could.

It came to the point where as soon as he touched my G-spot I would start to feel very engorged, so much so that I almost pushed his finger or penis out, and the pressure would keep on building and building. It had become an almost automatic response, as if a button had been pushed and then these sensations would begin to escalate. Being an understanding and attentive lover, and being so interested in helping me reach an intense orgasm, and G-spot type of orgasm, he did all he could to help me along. By talking to me and hugging me and holding me and reassuring me that it was okay to let go, nothing bad would happen and, in fact, it would probably feel very good and I should just allow myself to lose control and go for it!

One night it happened, along with a blood-curdling yell (he thinks I have a future in Hollywood horror movies). It caught us both unaware and unprepared, for not only did I have a G-spot orgasm but I also "ejaculated" liquid as I came to orgasm, soaking both him and the bed. I was freaked out by the experience and he was ecstatic (and we ended up changing the sheets at 2 o'clock in the morning). It was unlike any other orgasm I have had. While an orgasm usually has a very slow build-up with several plateau's, this one was more like an explosion with very intense sensations which would quickly subside. And, of course, there was usually some liquid ejaculate as well. Of course at first I did think I wet the bed, but after investigation we discovered this liquid was not urine, nor was it typical of female lubricant.

It seemed to have a scent and texture of its own-a nice pleasant smell, and very liquidly, more like water than any lubricating fluid generally emanating from the vaginal area.

It's only been a couple of months since we've discovered this new "treat". My lover enjoys it immensely and loves it when I "spray" him. He's hoping to replicate this phenomenon through oral stimulation but that somehow makes me uptight, but I know I'll eventually let go and let that happen as well. I now also seem to be multi-orgasmic when it comes to G-spot orgasms, I can have as many as my lover will give me, or as many as I want. After some initial foreplay consisting of kissing and touching, once I am aroused, all it takes is my lover putting his finger inside my vagina to start the process.

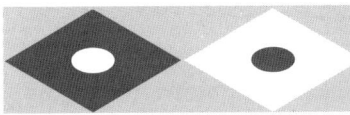

One of the best sexual positions for reaching G-Spot orgasms is the "Woman on top—reversed". Men's Health calls it Woman Astride, Facing Away "She's looking at your toes, stimulating your testicles or her clit. The principle advantage is the depth of penetration and the freedom of movement it affords. For even greater mobility, the woman can rise up and squat. Men's Health, page 153

Immediately upon feeling his finger enter my body, the engorgement and tightening feeling begins and all he has to do is rub the appropriate area a few times and I usually have a mind-blowing G-spot orgasm pretty quickly and it feels very, very good! A typical session would see me having eight to ten orgasms in as little as 10-15 minutes, however due to their physical intensity I do find them somewhat overwhelming and extremely exhausting. Although I do still ejaculate, it seems that the first two produce the most fluid, and the rest either have little fluid or are "dry". My lover has become extremely experienced in helping me achieve this number of orgasms and doesn't have to work too hard. In fact, sometimes while stimulating me (through intercourse or manually) all he has to do is whisper a few very special phrases into my ear, or plant a love-bite on the side of my neck and that is usually enough to bring me over the edge (and the orgasms definitely seem better if I can totally let go and vocalize as much as I want).

My final analysis is that with the right lover who is patient and attentive, a G-spot orgasm is within reach of all women, and it is definitely worth looking for. Although it does not replace the gentle climb and free fall of the conventional orgasm which I still enjoy immensely, it is a more intense deep orgasm which encompasses the whole body and which involves a total loss of control and the ability to let go and enjoy whatever happens. I actually see colors when I come.

My lover is thrilled that at 38 I have lost my "virginity" with him and I think it is because of him and his attention to detail, both physical and emotional, that I have been able to experience this new found sexual experience. Although he thinks I am an amazing woman due to my new sexual capacity, I think the credit is all his, for without his perseverance, patience and loving understanding, I don't think I would have been able to reach this new peak of sexual satisfaction.

*******Michaela 38 listener**

 Here are some suggestions made by the listeners to my radio show on how to reach and extend your ability to be orgasmic.

~I've got to be clenching my abdominal muscles to come. **Cindy**

~I can only come if I'm on my back and have complete reign to pump my legs up and down. This moves my clit so that I hit his pubic bone. It takes a bit of acrobatics but does it feel good when I get it! **Jane**

~If my boyfriend is taking too long to come, I moan in his ear and start moving my hand towards his asshole. Even me just trying to put a finger in there sends him completely over the edge! **Maggie**

 ~I have to use different sensations to make my girl come. If I give her oral sex between sips of a cold drink and a hot drink she's able to climax. I've been experimenting with mints, pop rocks, warm oil and whatever else can give her a safe sensation on her clit. It's the only thing that makes her climax. **Jake**

~I find that fantasy makes a big difference for me. If I can play out a scenario in my head, or we can talk sexy while he touches me, that helps me get over the hump. **MJ**

> **Sue's Tip:** Besides the usual Astoglide, Eros and KY jelly, my favorite lubricant is a plant mister. Some water with a drop of mineral oil mixed in works so well. Just spray to interesting parts or ask if he wants his "plant misted—mister...

 ~ Oral sex is the only thing that can make me come. I need about 15 minutes of tongue on my clit, no moving around to finally have it happen. **Janice**

~After not having an orgasm for decades, I have to start and stop with a sex toy while my husband is on top in order to have a climax. It's still not the kind you read about, where you can't talk afterwards, but it sure releases the sexual tension. I am so proud that I can finally do it. **Stella**

~ My boyfriend has never had a partner before me and  can't seem to come inside me. I found out that he masturbated with the inside of a glove and he loved the feel of the rabbit fur against his cock. I bought some rabbit pelts and use that on him. I also masturbate on it myself. He loves it! I would have never guessed if it hadn't come out of a conversation on your show. **Rhona**

~This may sound graphic but I found out how much guys fantasize about strap-on's and being fucked by talking to a stripper I know. She said that it was a common fantasy for guys to talk about with her. My boyfriend is really curious and all I have to do is bring up the subject and he gets totally turned on. **Debbie**

~I find that if my partner hums against my clit it can really send me. **Marcia**

Another Letter!

Dear Sue,

Great orgasms exists, this I know. My ex-wife had a lesbian affair during our (brief) marriage and learned about vaginal orgasms from her lover, and then she taught me. She had me masturbate her with two fingers, slapping my palm hard against her crotch. It took several minutes and damn near killed my arm, but she'd have orgasms the like of which I've never witnessed. Screaming out of control, her outbursts turned me into a wild animal of interest, when she'd orgasm this way it was like she was peeing. I don't know what blasted out of her vagina but it was like turning on a garden hose. It tasted very much like water, not unpleasant at all. Anyhow, that's how I know women have G-spots, and can cum if you give it to them they way they ask for it.

*****Malcolm 36

Dear Sue,

When I first started engaging in intercourse with my boyfriend (myself being 19 and he being 8 years older and more experienced), we were curious to find my G-spot. When he first told me what it was all about, I looked at him like he was crazy. Why would a woman want to feel as if they had to pee, then excrete fluid? For the past two and a half years we searched and tried to find this famous spot but were unsuccessful.

Another great vaginal orgasm position is one called "The Rear Window". The woman kneels down on the bed, supported by her elbows with hands clasped behind her head. As he enters from behind he supports himself by placing his hands on her shoulders. Contact is made in a particularly

The closest I ever got was having the major urge to push while my boyfriend was down on me but I held back in fear of urinating.

This past summer we found my G-spot without even searching for it; it just happened. My boyfriend and I were having intercourse, but he was also orally stimulating me back and forth. This time we were trying a position which we usually engage in but the angles of penetration were different. I was lying on my back with my feet up on his shoulders and then he pulled my butt higher up in the air, so I was in the bicycle position. From there he penetrated and orally stimulated me.

Then all of a sudden the urge to push feeling was there. I did, and usually nothing happens, but this time fluid came out. I was so embarrassed and shocked, but my boyfriend was supportive and told me not to hold back and just enjoy. There wasn't as much fluid excreted as there is now when he hits my G-spot.

The first couple of times when I excreted fluid I was very uneasy and didn't enjoy the orgasm

 as much. Recently when the famous spot is hit, several cups of fluid was excreted. We had two towels down but the bed sheet and the mattress still got soaked. It was unbelievable how much fluid was excreted. Even more fluid was excreted this past time and the orgasm was extremely intense.

- * * * * Deborah 23, listner

 Check out the website www.sexwithsue for more cool sex stuff

Here's a letter from a listener who experienced a gush of G-spot orgasms and worried that there was something wrong with her. As I mentioned earlier, many women who experience female ejaculation in conjunction with a G-spot (and mind blowing) orgasm can freak themselves right out!

Dear Sue,

You wanted to hear from women who have had amazing orgasms, G-spot and otherwise, well I am had one that was totally unforgettable. It happened to me when I was 21 years old, two years ago. My boyfriend and I were sleeping together away from home for the first time (we still live with our par-

 ents). We were at some of his friends' place in Quebec City. We stayed up late, just the two of us, to give each other massages with some very aromatic massage oil (the room must have smelled for days, and the mattress must still smell like oil!) We each took turns.

At one point, I was rubbing him all over and he fell asleep. I kept touching him and I realized this was really turning me on. Finally, I got on top of him and it woke him up. I was still on top of him, making love to him, when I felt some liquid running down my thighs. I asked him if he had come and he said no that it was I who was very wet. But by then the liquid had reached the sheets under my boyfriend's behind!

At that point I got REALLY scared! I got off him, terrified at what had happened, I put some clothes on and ran to the washroom. My boyfriend ran behind me laughing. He had smelled it and knew it wasn't his nor was it urine; I had "ejaculated".

I was very upset, my knees were trembling, I think I was even crying. It was a very frightening experience even though I had heard that it was possible for a girl to do that. Still, one part of me is always afraid that it will happen again, and another part of me hopes it will happen every night !

* * * * * **Kristie 24, listener**

Call your local radio station to see if Sue's syndicated show is on in your area!

Dear Sue,

While so many people consciously try to find their G-spot, I was fortunate to experience a G-spot orgasm purely by accident when I was in my late teens (though, I suspect my partner knew more about it than I did). The experience was so powerful that I can remember it in detail.

My family was away, and realizing the golden opportunity that had presented itself, my boyfriend and I could take our time making love. We were both very aroused and very relaxed. We were sitting on the floor and I was leaning against a sofa, with my legs bent upwards towards my chest. The position of my vagina was on a slight angle as he inserted his fingers inside me. The angle that he used was different, probably because of the way I was sitting and I was extremely aroused by watching him penetrate me with his fingers. He had a rhythm going as he moved his fingers with varying degrees of pressure. I found myself getting more and more aroused. We were kissing and fondling one another when all of a sudden his stroking hit a spot inside me. At first, it felt a little uncomfortable but that passed within a minute or so.

I remember telling my partner that it felt like amazing, but at the same time, I was afraid I was about to urinate. He reassured me by saying, "Just let yourself go." It was almost simultaneously with those words that this incredible intense feeling of excitement overcame my entire body. My body trembled and I felt a huge warm gush from inside of me. It felt like an electric current was running through my body! Underneath where I was sitting was an enormous puddle. I remember feeling embarrassed because I didn't know that a woman could ejaculate. Because it didn't appear to be the color or texture of vaginal discharge, I was certain it was urine. Although we figured he had hit my G-spot, it was only later, after reading about G-spots, that I understood what I had experienced. My partner was thrilled to be able to please me and felt a sense of pride from our "accomplishment" rather than discomfort.

You go girl!

Sometimes with other partners, the mission was not as successful which made me wonder. Indeed, there are obvious positive effects of finding a woman's G-spot, but there are negative effects of not finding it as well. It can be disappointing to both partners. What I have learned is that when the experience of finding a woman's g-spot is viewed by both partners as a process and not a goal, the outcome is better because the pressure is off. After all, most of the fun is getting there.

Because of the extreme power and intensity of a G-spot orgasm, it can be overwhelming both in emotional as well as physical terms. The trust and psychological connection I have felt with my partners was crucial in order for me to let myself go. While I can achieve multiple orgasms in lovemaking, the intensity of a G-spot orgasm is very draining and I seem to only be able to experience one at a time. I continue to have G-spot orgasms through manual stimulation, but there is not always ejaculation. I view my first G-spot experience as sexually empowering. In subsequent intimate relationships, I have found myself with increased confidence and a willingness to experiment.

* * * * * **Georgie** -listener

Dear Sue,

We are writing you to tell of our experiences with amazing orgasms. I had never had a vaginal orgasm before I met my current boyfriend. We had listened to your show together a number of times and the topic of the G-spot kept coming up. We were both curious (he more than I) and decided to see what it was all about.

The first time we tried was this summer. We did as you described, i.e., with me lying on my stomach and a pillow to raise my buttocks. Then palm down, he inserted his middle finger, applying a fairly strong pressure to what we both figured to be the spot (him by the description, me by the feeling that I had to go and pee.) After about ten minutes of this, I asked him to stop and was sure that I was going to pee all over, but he kept saying just give it a little longer. We continued for another twenty minutes or so, after which I insisted that he stop. He had mixed feelings about stopping, he said that he had felt a change in the size of the spot and figured that I must be really close, but on the other hand his finger was really sore. We stopped, promising that we would try again another day. The next day I felt like I had to pee every fifteen minutes or so (but each time I went, only a couple drops came out), while he felt like he had sprained his finger.

Two weeks later, after a great night of sex and both of us had just finished climaxing in the doggy style position, my boyfriend suggested that we go for the G-spot again. I was hesitant at first, but then he reminded me that you always say that it can take quite a number of attempts before a woman actually climaxes from stimulation of the G-spot. I stayed up on all fours and he started to perform oral sex on me and then inserted his finger up inside me to the spot. It felt really good and I had the feeling that I was going to pee but as he encouraged me to continue, within ten or fifteen minutes we were both surprised when a warm liquid spurted out all over his face.

 **Orgasm sometimes can be an elusive thing. Concerns about partner's satisfaction and orgasms are among the top five questions I get from my listeners. People are concerned that this problem is unique to them, but I keep hearing it from couples all over experiencing the same problems. The Durex Global Sex Survey, which is done every year, is consistent with other research. Between 20 to 25% of women struggle to get off.**

* * * * * **Chris**

Dear Sue,

This story is set in the late seventies in Florida. I was touring the country on my motorcycle after being dumped rather dramatically by the woman I'd been living with for several years. The trip was supposed to be a honeymoon but it didn't

> "The most common problem for women is orgasm, and their facility in bringing it about. About a quarter of the women I spoke to had never come, or weren't sure they had. About half were hamstrung that their orgasms were dependent on certain situations. Without their vibrator, or ex-husband, or the smell of gardenias at noon, they couldn't get off. Susie Bright, *Sexual State of the Union*, page 138

turn out that way. I'd already burned my bridges back home so I had no incentive not to take the trip anyway.

Several months after the start of the trip, a person I'd met introduced me to a girl he said would be just right for me.

He was right about that. I went to get a tire replaced, dropped in on her for coffee and disappeared for a week.

It was definitely lust at first sight, along with a "resonance" I hadn't felt before (or since). My friend didn't know whether to be worried or amused, and settled for bemused.

We had a lot in common - besides motorcycles, music and sex - and we were always relaxed with each other. There was no question that I would move in with her. We'd planned to be together for a long time...

The sex was great from the beginning. We were both in good shape, uninhibited and inventive. We'd make love four or five times a day and it wouldn't take a lot to get us "into the mood".

A Letter! Write Sue with your story....

So much for background...

Sometime during the first couple of weeks we were together, she made a big puddle in the bed. She was sure she'd had a childish accident and was unhappy and embarrassed about it. We showered and changed the sheets. She said it had happened before and resolved to empty her bladder before going to bed. She'd temporarily given up sex from sheer embarrassment the last time it happened, but neither one of us was THAT upset about it.

Her doctor had told her that the fluid was a bladder thing, and to go on a bland diet and give up sex and motorcycling for a while. Disaster!! She gave up motorcycling and we gave up intercourse (but not sex) and spicy food for a while. We were not very happy.

After a few weeks of this, it happened again - this time without intercourse. I had a couple of fingers inside her, being careful to avoid the urethra, and was stroking the labia around the clitoris and what later became known as the "Grafenberg spot". She liked that a lot, but when she orgasmed (for the third or fourth time) she wet the bed again. Disaster!!!

Now, I'm a fairly curious person and there was a lot of great sex at stake, so I did a little investigating while she was shamefacedly cleaning up the mess. The liquid was certainly NOT urine. It was not acidic and didn't develop that unmistakable odor so well known by urbanites. No one could explain it, but I was successful in convincing her that this was not a urinary problem, so we'd make sure we'd use a towel (whenever possible) and tried not to worry about it too much.

Since it hadn't hit the popular press yet (the book didn't  come out until after we were split up) we just accepted it as one of those things that make people unique; some people can impersonate farm animals, she could do it for fountains!

After a while, either from accommodation or changing techniques, this was only a "problem" every couple of weeks. I put problem in quotations because it was one of those things which she really enjoyed although it WAS a bit messy. You certainly wouldn't want to do it in polite company!

By comparison, it was way less messy than sex during menstruation and we tolerated that well enough.

Kevin 46 ****

Dear Sue,

I had been married for 20 years and had sex with a few other partners before that, after all it was the 70's and things were different

"One of my most quoted lines is, "I never met a man who told me he didn't know how to come, or didn't know where his penis was." That pretty much sums up the dilemma of women's sexual response. Susie Bright, *Sexual State of the Union,* page 138

100

then. When my marriage broke up in 1994 I had not had any sexual relations for about four years before that. Afterwards, I had a couple of flings (and it was safe sex) but while I enjoyed sex I never ever thought it could be the way it is now.

Dave and I seem to be a perfect match. It did take a bit of time for us to trust each other, we both had come from abusive marriages, yes, as you well know men are abused too. But right from the first time we made love, it was fantastic. We were both a bit taken aback by it but we sure weren't going to knock it.

Then one night it happened, I had the most out of this world orgasm I had ever had. We listen to your show and from all the feelings it seemed to be a G-spot orgasm. We went to your web site and read up on it and sure enough it was. I was very curious about it since it was so strong so a few days later when we were alone we did some exploring. Dave took my finger and placed it on my G-spot and helped me to have another one.

Since then we have found ways for me to have one with different positions, me lying on my tummy and him entering from behind works very well and of course he can do it with his fingers at anytime. I don't produce as much fluid as you say some women do but I do get very wet.

- *** * * * Donna 47**

Hear excerpts from my radio show on www.sexwithsue.com. Send me your penis stories. Let's make Mr. Happy famous!

Dear Sue,

My wife and I were listening to your radio program on Sunday evening, your topic that evening was "How to locate the G-spot". It all started on our couch, you were describing how to find the G-spot to the people calling in on the show. At that time my wife and I started to get turned on more and more. I started kissing her on the neck and slowly rubbing her clitoris, this got us very excited, I inserted one finger in her vagina and moving my finger like saying "come here", after several minutes, my wife said let's move this to the bedroom, where it's more comfortable. We were touching each other and getting turned on like never before. Finally, I got on top of her, my very sexy partner, and inserted my penis and started to pump faster and faster. She had an orgasm, but then she said to me, "It's not feeling like Sue said on the radio, that a G-spot orgasm feels like having to pee."

Sue Says: Remember, very few women can come from straight intercourse. Even the pounding G-Spot stimulation which can feel great, learning to come vaginally takes time, experience and work. Don't give up!

So she got on top of me and inserted my penis into her vagina and after a while she started to say "Oh yes, oh yes, I'm starting to feel like I have to pee". I grabbed her butt and we started to pump together faster and faster and at that moment she started to scream and it started to flow out of her like never before.

We wet all the sheets on the bed, and I was wet from the belly button to my knees.

P.S. If it was not for the "Sex with Sue" program on the radio we would never have had the wonderful experience. Thank you Sue! Keep up the good work.

- * * * * **Darren 35** ****

Dear Sue,

For me, the orgasms that I ejaculate with are always more intense, almost an altered state. It takes a long time, it usually takes several orgasms to build up to it and it always seems to be associated with a vaginal orgasm. Or, I should say a series of them.

- * * * * **Leanne 36**

Dear Sue,

I had one partner during college who seemed to ejaculate. This woman was amazing. The times when she would noticeably ejaculate were after long periods of heightened arousal without orgasm. Most of the time she would cum quickly and frequently, but once in a while we would both delight in having me torment her orally, digitally and

"Women ask, "How can I come? How can I come more easily? How can I come at all? Even though only 13% of the women polled said they had never experienced orgasm, from the questions it seemed that half the women in the crowd were orgasmically frustrated in one way or another. Yikes! Talk about sublimated anger. Women asked where their G-spots were, and how they could ejaculate. It is such a female sex question, to be searching for your sex: WHERE IS IT, WHERE IS IT? Men don't have this location problem. Susie Bright. Sexual State of the Union, sometimes with fisting as well. If she could hold off for long enough (45 minutes or more) she would have an incredibly intense orgasm accompanied by ejaculation. The fluid issued was watery, but thicker than urine and had very little similarity in smell and taste to urine.

* * * * * Jeremy

Dear Sue,

I am a 24 year-old married woman! My husband and I have an excellent sex life and plan on having it for a long time to come. Which leads to my story about my first G-spot orgasm!

While my husband and I were dating, we used to have a night reserved just for us. We called it "Ritual Thursday". It was a night we would hibernate in the basement at his mom's house. We would explore each other during the time between our TV shows.

On one of our "Ritual Thursday's", my boyfriend was performing oral sex on me with one finger inside my vagina when I suddenly felt the urge to urinate! I decided to ignore it because I was feeling too good. As the tension grew, my urge to urinate started to go away. After about 15 minutes, my whole body released and I felt very wet, so wet that the sheets on the spare bed also got wet! I was so

The P spot is the male equivalent of the G-spot. More and more butt plugs and strap-on toys seem to be selling to couples according to my friend Daryl Brown, President of Calston Industries. They manufacturer some of the best sex toys in the world, and say that anal play is becoming increasingly popular among heterosexual couples.

embarrassed and thought if I pretended not to notice the wetness, my boyfriend wouldn't say anything! This started to happen all the time and I thought there was something with me. I thought that I had lost bladder control and was urinating every time my boyfriend performed oral sex on me! I was embarrassed and wouldn't let my boyfriend perform oral sex on me anymore! I came up with every excuse possible. So to make a long story short, I continued to allow my boyfriend to perform oral sex and I kept what I thought was urinating, and I kept ignoring it and I just told myself that it couldn't possibly be bothering my boyfriend because he would have said something. I just told myself that I had a hard time controlling my bladder. I now realize that what I thought was a bladder control problem, was actually a G-spot orgasm. I don't find that it feels any different then a clitoral orgasm, it's just a more intense feeling!

'Boys and girls are crazy about anal stimulation because it feels really good. It stimulates the prostate gland on men and the internal clitoral body on women. Both of these kind of stimulation can propel one to orgasm. Susie Bright, Sexual State of the Union, page 144.

* * * * * **Elaina**

Putting it all together

Mind Blowing, Toe Curling orgasms that turn you to jello need not be elusive. For men, the ability to control your ejaculation and stay at an orgasmic plateau is shown to be a matter of doing the work it takes to be a super-lover. (able to leap bedposts in a single bound). For women, reaching orgasm effortlessly, and learning to climax from stimulation to your cervix and G-spot should be something you can add to your sexual repertoire. It's a lot about training your body, getting the information, and trying different things. And I think it's about not giving up and allowing yourself the permission to fantasize and really let go with your partner. They say that the most common fear of North Americans is public speaking. For many people the fear of  looking ridiculous risk taking in the bedroom is much scarier than talking in front of a roomful of people. David Schnarrch, the well known marital therapist claims that taking risks sexually with your partner is the single biggest thing you can do to create intimacy between you. I happen to agree, and if you get silly and wild, magically things happen. It's about really good, satisfying sex.

Everyone wants to know if the couple next door are having better, crazier and more orgasmic sex than they are. That's why I've included so many real-life listener stories in this book. If you've got an incredible orgasm story that offers others suggestions on how to get there for themselves, I would like to hear from you. Please e-mail me at **www.sexwithsue.com**, and tell me your orgasm or story about a penis you may be fond of for my upcoming book Giant Phalluses: Everything you ever wanted to know about Penis Size. Men that I speak to want to last longer, go again, continue defying gravity with rock hard erections.

Women, it seems just want to get off regularly without having to sacrifice a chicken to reach one, or have it take 60 minutes of coaxing to finally come. Having incredible orgasms are a wonderful extra.

As a sex broadcaster, I speak with hundreds of people every week, and what I've learned is that the ability to have orgasms is something we all have the ability to learn. Sex although the second most basic need in the human body (after food), and is natural and necessary, is also a learned behavior. Think of it as learning to snowboard. It takes a while for your body to learn the moves, but once you get it you never forget and the feeling is amazing.

The final word is about fantasy. Don't be afraid to send your mind off on an adventure with Arnold Schwartzenager or Cindy Crawford or whomever or whatever turns you on. Jimmy Carter called fantasy unfaithful in his heart, but I strongly disagree. Fantasy only brings you closer as a couple, gets you more in touch with your sexual self, and allows those Quivering Jello orgasms to happen. Susie Bright says about great orgasms, "Give someone a map, a helpful book, a video for fantasies and then wait for the gushing thank you letters." Fantasies are the wild card. "In an erotically charged situation, your panties may be bunched up, or your arm falling asleep but you still come like gangbusters. If however, your mind doesn't feel desire, you can have every hole filled, every vibration in place, and still be completely unmoved." (Susie Bright, *Sexual State of the Union*, page 139)

These orgasms are worth chasing. Learn the curve, carve the mountain, and lay like a Quivering pile of Jello at the end of the run. Good Luck!

Get Ready For UNZIPPED, The amazing new Television Series!

UNZIPPED... sex ed...With teeth!

Unzipped is an edgy, often raw, yet always enjoyable exploration of everyone's favorite topic - **SEX**!
Much of the strength of the show comes from its strong emsemble:
Sue McGarvie, renowned Canadian author and host of the syndicated radio program 'Sunday Night Sex with Sue';
Cogee, the cool, yet hot, American comedian and rapper, who exudes GQ with soul; and
Teddy Wilson, the hilarious and very relatable prankster and former child actor on Canada's 'You Can't Do that on Television'.
Together, their charisma and chemistry melt away our audience's inhibitions and pull the viewer into an intimate discussion of sex-related topics.

Our audience can live vicariously through Sue's uninhibited approach to sex-related issues and, through their exploration, they will discover new areas of interest and excitement.

Unzipped combines everyone's natural curiosity about how, where, and how often everyone else is 'getting it on' with regular flashes of comic brilliance. **Unzipped** is being co-produced by Kari Lynn Robinson (Cause She Can Productions) and Jeff Boulton (Dante Entertainment), with Lillyann Goldstein and Sue McGarvie the Executive Producers.

the bug show
erotica & pornography
sexual trends
kama sutra
fantasies
aphrodisiacs
senior sex
the vagina show
the penis show
swinging
fetishes
keeping it hot
being single

13 Half-Hour Episodes

For more information on **Unzipped** please contact the producers at:
Tel: (416) 534-6728
Fax: (416) 534-4792
E-mail: production@unzipped.tv

**About the Author:
Sue McGarvie– Sex with Sue
International Sex Therapist Broadcaster, Author, Syndicated Talk Show host - Radio and Television**

Sue's professional training is in psychology and reproductive medicine, and she has been a registered Sex Therapist since 1992. She is the founder of The Ottawa Sex Therapy Clinic and is a member of The Society of Obstetricians and Gynecologists of Canada, The Canadian Urology Association, The Federation of Medical Women, and The Sex Therapy Council of Canada. Sue is also the author of two books on sexuality and as a sex expert she has been an expert witness, insurance industry consultant, pharmaceutical and government lobbyist and a professional speaker. She was nominated for the Rotman's Canadian Women Entrepreneur for 2002, and is a Top 40 under 40 finalist.

Beginning in 1993, Sue hosted a #1-rated radio call-in show for five years called *Sunday Night Sex With Sue* with Standard Broadcasting on The Bear CKQB in Ottawa. She has since gone on to produce a 90 second syndicated radio series called *Sexual Solutions* which runs on stations internationally across Canada and into the US. She has just finished a new television series called *Unzipped* that will air throughout North America in the spring of 2003. Her new full hour Sex with Sue radio show will also launch at that time.

Beginning in 1999, Sue founded **Passion Media**, a multimedia company marketing mainstream, tasteful sexuality and relationships throughout North America. Sue helped take the company public in July of 2002. Sue is the media spokesperson about sex on countless shows including Penn and Teller's new Showtime series, and for the Durex Global Sex Surveys.

Sue wrote the applications and lobbied the CRTC for two national digital television licenses which were granted in December 2000 for *Passion Television* and *The Singles Network*. A third specialty channel is expected to be licensed and launched in 2004.

Sue McGarvie has been named a Woman of Distinction (1997), the I. H. Asper Broadcast Entrepreneur of the Year (1998), and Business and Professional Women's Association Woman of the Year (1994). She is also the 2002 Women in the Spotlight Award-winner for volunteer of the year for her work as National Mentorship Director with Wired Women, and the 2003 winner of the Canadian Women in Communications (CWC) prestigious Volunteer of the Year Award.

Sue sits on the National mentorship Committee for The Canadian Women in Communications member of The International Alliance for Women, and International Women's Forum, and has established an International Mentorship Database. She is a national corporate director with a number of boards including UNIFEM—part of The United Nations Association of Canada, The Juvenile Diabetes Research Foundation Campaign Cabinet, and the new Shirley E. Greenberg Women's Health Center at The Ottawa Hospital. Sue has been a corporate director for a few start-ups in her work as a Mentor and with women entrepreneurs.

Sue stays sane and grounded with the help of a supportive husband, two blue-eyed kids, and a sense of humor.

Sue "Sex with Sue" McGarvie
International Sex Expert and Therapist
Syndicated radio and television host
99 Holland Ave., Suite 105,
Ottawa, Ontario K1Y 0Y1
Canada
(613) 725-2789   www.sexwithsue.com
sexwithsue@rogers.com